Norwegian Mittens
and Gloves

ANNEMOR SUNDBØ

Norwegian Mittens and Gloves

TRAFALGAR SQUARE
North Pomfret, Vermont

First published in the United States of America in 2011 by
Trafalgar Square Books
North Pomfret, Vermont 05053

Originally published in Norwegian as *Norske vottar og vantar*
by Norske Samlaget, Oslo

ISBN: 978-1-57076-495-0
Library of Congress Control Number: 2011929196

Photography by Tove Breistein, except pages 7, 8, 9, 14, 15, 156 by
Annemor Sundbø
Pattern charts by Søre Netterstrøm
Interior design by Beate Syversen
Cover design by RM Didier

Printed in China

10 9 8 7 6 5 4 3 2 1

Table of Contents

Foreword

One day in 1983, I became the owner of a shoddy mill with almost 1000 different mittens. I had actually set out to have six months practical experience at the Torridal Tweed and Wool Comforter Factory in Kristiansand but the old mill owner would only agree to train me if I promised one thing: I had to buy the factory first!

I was a weaving instructor now given a new opportunity in life – to manage the old production equipment for recycling knitted waste. I would run the last remaining shoddy mill in Norway. The building was full of old sacks that held more than 16 tons of wool fabrics. Shoddy is the English word for "rags" and sjoddi was the Norwegian industry term for recycled wool. Such "rag mills" were common up to the end of the twentieth century. One fed the machine with worn-out sweaters, socks, hand coverings, underclothes – no wool remnants were too worn and no threads too small to be recycled. Out of the machines came a grey tweedy fiber mass that was used to fill mattresses, comforters, and sleeping bags. If the fiber quality was good enough, the fibers could be spun into tweed, wool rug and blanket yarns.

A wool fabric remnant has been turned into soles, a footstep with a guiding star that points back into our knitting history.

7

I had the choice of shredding or saving a vast wealth of patterns.

It didn't take many days before I realized what an enormous amount of knitting history had been thrown into those sacks. I started putting aside items that I thought had one story or another to tell. With support from the Norwegian Cultural Council, I managed to go through all the layers of raw materials in my hunt for cultural treasures.

Today I am once again sitting near a knitting collection that weighs about one ton. The garments represent everything that has been worn on the body, from the outermost to innermost layers, from local and national traditions, and which also have lead threads out into the world and back into time.

I want to bring threads and skeins back out from this private collection and my experiences to narrate some of the stories from the pattern traditions that have wandered into our knitting culture.

MOOSE AT SUNDOWN

When I was a little girl I used all the yarn leftovers I could find to knit doll clothes. On my childhood bed I had a "Moose at Sundown" coverlet with motifs formed by small loops, a pile weaving. It was easy to draw out yarn from the coverlet. If I pulled out every other thread, the pattern didn't completely disappear. I then decided to take out the little motifs on the coverlet. After a while the blanket was threadbare. My recycling efforts weren't really appreciated at that time because, after a while, the sun disappeared, the moose was unrecognizable, and the conifer forest became quite sparse on my decorative weaving. Thirty years later I stood at a machine with a huge metal drum covered with sharp steel teeth for shredding up woolen garments.

After a while I saw what fabulously rich designs were being lost in the shredding machine, and it gradually occurred to me that I was on the way to eradicating an important part of knitting history and pattern traditions. I stood with garments in my hands that had been made with thousands of women's hands in countless work hours over the past century. It wasn't just their durability that distinguished these garments. Out of almost every single sack I pulled out small pattern motifs, border panels, and figures—animals, plants, dancers, and symbols of energy sources such as the sun, moon, and stars. It occurred to me that the storerooms were not only burial mounds filled with knitted waste but also a treasure chest full of knitting traditions from ordinary life in our folk culture, knitting traditions encapsulating our recent past, but which didn't have any other value at that point in time than as raw materials for factory products. Pattern figures such as moose, reindeer, dogs and birds steadily surfaced. A hunting instinct awakened in me and I decided to capture as many animals as possible from my rag pile.

I stood there holding the thread of fate in my hands: which pieces should live on and which should be thrown back into the piles for stuffing? I understood that my choices would have consequences for our knitting history. I also felt that the pattern figures had a sort of soul. It was as if there were messages or whisperings of small secret codes from the past. Was there a "transmigration of souls" from the older pattern culture? Were the pattern motifs a legacy from a time when the symbols and pictures added energy with magic, mythic, cosmic, and astrological power? Even if the embellishments were just to please the eyes, I felt that the language of design in the knitted garments also imparted a deeper meaning. The embellishment and pattern combinations weren't simply accidental.

Universal Language

I began to contemplate the proverb about "disappearing like a spirit in the rag pile." Did the sym-

One of the trophies programmed into my knitting machine.

I don't think the pattern combinations were accidental.

One of the oldest knitting finds in Europe. Mafalda, a member of the Spanish royal family who was buried in 1275, had his head lying on this pillow.

bols and picture motifs have some sort of energy, a magical and spiritual power? Would it be possible to conjure out this spirit? In order to find the answer about whether the embellishments had some meaning beyond the aesthetic, I began researching written sources about different cultures, religions, and folk beliefs.

Europeans used animal figures and symbolic markings long before they were transformed into knitting techniques. With the Templar Knights and crusades a system of codes for coats of arms were put into place. Knowledge of the signs and symbols, or heraldry, developed. Heraldry is an interesting mixture of the symbolic and the decorative that we inherited from the crusaders of the 11-13th centuries but that originated in the distant past, about 4000-3000 years before Christ in Mesopotamia and Babylon – in today's Iraq and, according to the Bible, humanity's birthplace.

By using repetitions, mirror imaging and patterns repeating in width and length, symbols became ornaments. In folk beliefs, reverse imaging and repetition are ways to imbue symbols with increased strength and divine power. Many pattern figures are found in different religions but what they symbolize varies and is adapted to the particular belief. The earliest European knitting find that has been preserved is from 1275. Two pillows were found in graves in the town of Burgos in northern Spain, that were covered with a pattern mixture from Muslim, Christian and heraldic traditions. The border contains Arabic script, an Islamic blessing, as well as birds, stars, rosettes, and lilies – some of the very same motifs that we knit on Norwegian mittens today.

The patterns that appeared later are Spanish and Italian and are related to those from the Orient and Asia. These would have followed the routes of the old Silk Road from China. It is very interesting to be able to follow the figures on their wandering around the globe through thousands of years. It clearly shows that, over a long time and through many places, people have made a common journey unaffected by time, race, or latitude.

Most of the motifs are an inheritance from a time when not everyone could read so the language of pictures was an important means of communication. With the help of patterns and figures one could awaken thinking, arouse sensations, and generate associations, without having to be there one's self. The symbol could fire up the imagination and convey ideas and feelings regardless of one's spoken language and taboos.

FOLK BELIEFS AND FOLK ART

From the beginnings of the Norwegian textile culture folk beliefs and superstitions were a part of daily life. The visible and the invisible worlds lived side by side and the powers of nature, light and dark, were personified as fairies, pixies, and trolls that lived near or even among the Nordic gods and Christian beliefs. In order to better understand these spiritual beliefs of our forebears we also need to know a little about the living situation in the past. We must try to place ourselves within concepts and values people lived with before it was common to turn on the light with a switch on the wall. People needed protection from the dark and the unknown and guiding stars showed the way. This explains why eight-pointed stars were often found on mittens, knitted nightshirts, and pillows. It was customary in the middle ages to bury the dead in knitted nightshirts with the head resting on a pillow with eight-pointed stars. Night symbolized everything that was dark, unknown and dangerous. Winter was the night of the year and death ruled the night.

From the earliest times, art expressed itself decoratively with shapes and colors. The primitive man decorated himself with war and hunting trophies and shining amulets to distinguish himself in battle or to impress the enemy and, of course, to impress the opposite sex. Animals have been used as motifs as far back as in the cave paintings made by the Cro-Magnon people 20,000-30,000 years ago.

We have worked figures into Norwegian knitted garments for about 200 years. These patterns are now regarded as particularly Norwegian knitting motifs and national symbols but the motifs can be found all over the world in various textile techniques. The range of patterns for knitting has been stylized and adapted for the technique. The language of design varies from palms, doves and pinecones in southern Europe to eight-pointed stars, spruce branches and reindeer in the north. The symbolic meanings are also similar, even if the motifs come from different geographic areas. They relate to uprisings, victories, paradise, and eternal life; they concern love, fertility and protective signs against dangers.

The patterns that Norwegians today would call typically Norwegian, can be found in the oldest pattern books from Italy, Switzerland, France, and Germany dating back to the sixteenth to eighteenth centuries. The motifs in these pattern books were not newly created at that time but were older designs that the art of book printing made possible to spread more widely.

Forms of the motifs were adapted to local folk art and textile techniques thus becoming distinct. Terms such as "Norwegian knitting" and "Selbu knitting" have become ingrained in people's consciousness. We include the moose, deer, and reindeer among our national symbols. Why has "Norwegian knitting" become an internationally-recognized concept for two-color pattern knitting when the patterns were originally not particularly Norwegian?

The animal motifs I found in my rag pile seem to come from the first half of the twentieth century and were knitted in the districts and valleys around the mills, mainly in Agder province. Many of the deer figures are accompanied by a spruce tree, a sun, and a dog. Some are featured with other motifs that can be interpreted as a spring, a girl, or an olive branch. The same figures are found in medieval cross stitch embroidery and weavings, as well as samplers from the eighteenth and nineteenth centuries. Samplers were a type of swatch, part of the curriculum for learning embroidery that young girls practiced.

Animal motifs can be found in many forms and are charted in the earliest printed pattern books. They wandered through most textile techniques until they were featured in knitting patterns from the eighteenth century up to our own time. Deer were depicted alongside water or a running brook in a spruce forest with a large, red glowing sun in the background. Animal motifs were fashionable in Norwegian knitting of the 1930's and "moose at sundown" paintings and woven tapestries were popular. The only explanation I can come up with for this style is that people considered so many of the animals as our national animals and they wanted something typically Norwegian.

After 1905 and the dissolution of the union with Sweden our national symbols became important for profiling our country and setting a standard for our cultural heritage and Norwegian uniqueness. Norway's Handcraft hired two young, newly graduated textile artists, Annichen Sibbern and Elsa Poulsson to collect knitting patterns from all around the country and to publish them in book form. Annichen Sibbern published the book, Norske Strikkemønstre (*Norwegian Knitting Patterns*) in 1929 and Elsa Poulsson published Charted Patterns for Knitting and Embroidery in 1947.

Annichen Sibbern's book was later published in English as *Norwegian Knitting Designs* and has recently been reprinted in the U.S. The book sold a total of 78,000 copies and is considered the most important factor contributing to the international concept of "Norwegian Knitting."

LOCAL TRADITIONS AND THE INTERNATIONAL CONCEPT

The knitting patterns that Annichen Sibbern based her book on were taken from older knitted garments from various places in the country, while Elsa Poulsson used many motifs from samplers or stylized the motifs herself for the charted patterns so they could be easily knit. These patterns had been living in Norwegian local textile traditions in the nineteenth century. In the previous century there had been little pattern knitting. Knitting first came on the scene in Norway after a war and trade restrictions in the early nineteenth century. Perhaps we should thank Napoleon for the blockade and halt to imports that forced Norwegians to produce goods for their own use with their own raw materials. Patterns were adapted from elegant foreign clothing embellished with motifs from the universal language of symbols.

Up until 1814 and the split from Denmark, Norwegian folk costumes were fashioned after European styles that swept through towns and commercial centers. Earlier our country had been swamped with cheap imported knitted goods that Danish peddlers bought in quantity in Jutland and then sold in Norway. Customs' records from that period reveal that the imported exclusive knitted silk nightshirts were most often decorated with eight-pointed stars.

In all those ways, influences wandered in over our borders and then moved from town to town. By the time Norway was independent, there was a widespread desire to use our own raw materials rather than imported goods. There were continual newspaper debates concerning the notion that importation of unnecessary goods should be limited as should unnecessary luxury. Norwegian independence had to be cultivated and love for our country came first.

In the course of the nineteenth century, Norwegian folk costumes became increasingly significant.

Their wealth of colors identified their connections to specific districts and valleys. At the same time, knitting was more often used for clothing that was antecedent to today's classic knitted garments. We "Norwegianize" imported knitted goods by adding in elements and motifs from our own traditions but we also cast a side glance at luxurious foreign clothing. There was competition to lead in the international arena. Ethnic and folk art was important so that our country could present itself as unique, but also to show the differences between the Norwegians and Swedes in the fight to dissolve the union. Handcraft work should contribute to and defend Norway's honor.

In the first world exhibition in London in 1851, everything from machines to raw materials to finished products from every country was displayed. A catalogue from the London exhibit listed knitted goods, with 26 different named patterns form Shetland, one of which was called "the Armada Cross." This seems to be the origin of the myth that the crew from a ship in the Spanish Armada that wrecked on one of the small islands outside Shetland, Fair Isle, in 1588, taught the islanders how to knit. No knitted garment has been preserved from the 300 years following the shipwreck on this tiny island, Fair Isle, but, nevertheless, the myth developed and a single color pattern on a multicolor background would forever afterwards be designated "Fair Isle" knitting in knitting lexicons. The crew of the Spanish Armada would have come from both the Baltics and the Basque region of Spain. Where had those sailors gotten their knitting traditions?

KNITTING ART AND MASS PRODUCTION

No other knitting style has been as popular in Norway as "Selbu knitting." I have a collection of more than 1000 different mittens and gloves that are connected to the Selbu tradition. As happened with the tiny island of Fair Isle, the town of Selbu in Norway is the namesake of a knitting style that has grown larger than the tradition which originally developed in this Trøndelag town.

Selbu lies on the road between Trondheim and Sweden which meant that many new influences passed through the area. The town produced millstones and had some large and powerful businesses. For centuries commercial routes ranged

An example of a mitten pattern published by Husfliden (Norwegian Craft Association) in the early 20th century (drawing marked as no. 94, and signed A. H.).

out from the Swedish border to the continent via the Baltic Sea, through Jämtland and Härjedalen and over to the Russian rivers. The Caucasus, Armenia, and Turkey seem to have been the richest sources of patterns deriving from both the Byzantine and Christian cultures. Motifs such as the lily, carnation and tulip came from that region. The "rosettes" of these motifs evolved into "roses" given several local names in Selbu knitting.

Marit Gulsetbrua Emstad, also known as "the mother of Selbu knitting," deserves the honor for insuring that Selbu denotes a particular concept in international knitting terminology. She was born in 1841 and was the first knitter to sell mittens with the "Selbu rose," or eight-pointed star, to Husfliden in Trondheim in 1897. When she was thirteen years old she began collecting knitting patterns. She had rich sources to choose from: wood carvings, coverlet weaving, and embroidery. The town was especially well known for white work embroidery, an Italian technique (tala tagliata) that must

The Selbu mitten spread widely – even to Estonia, as shown by this weekly magazine from 1938.

have been a rich pattern source. In Trondheim, this technique was called "Selbu embroidery."

These patterns were easily adapted to knitting. Before 1900 pattern work was mostly used on textiles for home use and as gifts. For wedding preparations, one had to make mittens and gloves that the bride would give out to the guests during the celebration. They were personal gifts that often had knitted-in pattern symbols, initials and dates. They included vast amounts of different pattern combinations and are a rich source for inspiration.

We Norwegians are not alone in picking up patterns and adapting them to knitting techniques. Our neighboring states have done likewise, particularly in the Baltic countries (Estonia, Latvia, and Lithuania) where they use numerous color combinations and knitting techniques. The book, *Finnish Knitted Ornaments*, written by Theodor Schrint in 1895 contains many of "our" Selbu patterns. The dog we call a "buhund" or elkhound in Norwegian knitting is called a Karelian dog or Lapphound in Finland.

One of the most typical Selbu mitten motifs, a reindeer, was recorded in Mary Thomas's knitting book from 1938 as Lithuanian. Older traditional gloves from Lithuania never had animal figures but reindeer and moose motifs were very popular in all the Nordic countries between the two world wars. They appeared in all the women's magazines, often with the same pictures, and were very stylish in every Nordic country.

The motifs we now designate as Selbu patterns can be found in several textile techniques. Cross stitch embroidered samplers contained many of the most common motifs, such as crosses, anchors, hearts, wreaths, flowers, evergreen

14

branches, tree of life, birds, deer, stars, rosettes, roses, hourglasses, dogs, leaves, men, women, lines of dancers, letters, numbers, and initials with crowns.

The patterns received personal and local names in Selbu, such as "Emstad-rose," "Kolset-rose," "Lundbek-rose," "Hoem's rose" and "Vold-set-rose," or a dialect name such as "vêrhonrrose" (because the top of the petals bend like a ram's horn), "endløs-rosa" (endless rose – because the pattern parts can be endlessly expanded in width and height), "sjennrosa" (star rose – eight-pointed star), "tell-rosa" (pine rose, pine branch rose) and "skatroll" (beetle).

What really transformed Selbu knitting into an international concept was a knitters' association. An organized home industry between the wars exported over 100,000 pairs of gloves and mittens a year to all the winter sports countries in the world, as well as countless numbers of patterned hats, sweaters, and stockings. Around two thousand knitters produced items to sell during that time. At the beginning of the 1920's Selbu Handcraft Central and "Mitten Central" sent Selbu designs out onto the world market. Several other home industry networks made gloves and mittens with similar patterns and sold them around Norway in tourist shops and handcraft stores.

My grandmother knitted many different reindeer sweaters. My grandfather and grandmother's cousin, Inga, wearing their sweaters. Grandmother is behind the camera.

KNIT YOUR OWN REINDEER!
The original mittens I have chosen to rework for patterns in this book have been darned, patched, and felted after extensive wear. They were constructed following mitten designs that might have been published in leaflets, books, weekly magazines, or patterns that went from hand to hand. I have written missing pattern instructions, adjusted the sizing on hands and thumbs that were dispro-portioned, and used as inspiration for new designs some "store-bought mittens" that might be copy-righted.

My grandmother knitted several garments with reindeer in the 1930s. She said that many women came to her and asked for her patterns. But all were turned away and told to make their own reindeer! I hope that you will be inspired to create your own variations and combinations using the motifs I found in the rag pile. In the spirit of my grandmother, I hope that everyone who loves knitting will embellish their garments with the animal motifs and knit in their own spirit.

15

Basic techniques

by Terri Shea

BEFORE YOU BEGIN

When you are going to knit mittens and gloves, you follow certain ground rules: knit and purl stitches, increasing and decreasing, knitting with two colors. If you are familiar with these terms and know how to do them, then you can begin to knit.

If you have never knit mittens or gloves before, it's a good idea to begin by knitting a pair of single color mittens first. There are loads of easy patterns available. If you've never knit with two colors, you should begin with a pattern that has a two-color knit cuff. Knitting two-color designs on a cuff is good practice for learning how tightly the yarn must be held so that you get the correct gauge for knitting in the round. Pattern knit cuffs can also become a pair of pretty wrist warmers. In that case, finish the same way as you began, with a few rounds of ribbing before binding off.

Whenever yarn floats on the wrong side are long (across more than about 4 stitches), the stranded yarn can be twisted once around the yarn you are knitting with. Make sure that the strands don't pull in.

ANATOMY OF A MITTEN

A classic Norwegian mitten is a masterpiece of knitting. The classic graphic pattern combines perfectly with the shape of our hands. When you have understood how the mitten or glove is constructed you can create any pattern combination imaginable in any size and with any yarn.

CUFFS

A Norwegian mitten always begins at the cuff and is then knit up to the tips of the fingers. There is no one way to cast on so you can use the method you prefer. Cuffs are usually about 3¼-4 in / 8-10 cm long for adults and 2½-3¼ in / 6-8 cm long for children.

RIBBING FOR CUFF

The ribbing should have about 70-80% the number of stitches as for the hand. For the most part, ribbing is k2/p2 with symmetrical contrast color stripes at the center. The ribbing should fit a little tightly around the wrist, which is very practical for wearing with jackets that have narrow sleeves. Ribbing can be used on all mittens and is particularly appropriate for children's mittens that will be worn for playing outside in the snow.

PATTERN KNIT CUFFS

Generally pattern-knit cuffs feature borders with motifs different from those in the main pattern on the back of the hand although a simpler motif on the cuff is often repeated on the thumb. The pattern-knit cuff often has a border with stars, endless roses, dancers or acanthus scrolls. There might also be another simple border above and below the main pattern border. The stitch count must be correct for the pattern on the cuff and increased in such a way that it works for the pattern on the body of the mitten. Formerly most mittens or gloves with pattern-knit cuffs were made for men.

LACE CUFFS

Lace cuffs have a very feminine look. The most typical lace is a wave pattern. You can knit lace by making a hole with a yarnover and then knitting 2 stitches together. Usually lace cuffs are longer than those with a ribbed border, and are striped to emphasize the wave pattern. Lace cuffs require fewer stitches than other knit stitch cuffs because the pattern makes them more elastic.

GAUNTLET CUFFS / FISHTAIL CUFFS

Gauntlet cuffs / Fishtail cuffs are less common these days but have a particularly elegant shape and can be very fine for wearing with a folk costume and other traditional outfits. In earlier times gauntlet mittens were worn on a belt with the tail ("a star" or "fishtail") displayed at the front.

PATTERN KNITTING

There are different patterns on the back of the hand and the palm and in between is a dividing line. On newer mittens, often knit with a heavier yarn, this line is usually only one stitch wide but on older mittens it might be knitted over three stitches with "lice." I call that border "dancing ants" or little ants that march over the hands. Another popular version is a two-stitch line with alternating black and white stitches forming oblong blocks.

THUMB GUSSET

Mittens often have a thumb gusset with its own pattern that matches perfectly with the rest of the mitten. You begin at the base of the hand with three stitches, and then increase on every other round – or on every third or fourth round depending on the gauge – at the same time you stagger the colors for the typical block pattern. When this pattern is wide enough to fit across the thumb, stop increasing and place the stitches on a holder or piece of yarn. Because you've increased 8-10 or more stitches the thumb gusset widens to follow the shape of your hand below the thumb.

For most of the patterns in this book, I've moved the stitches from the thumb gusset onto a holder and then cast on enough new stitches so that the stitch count for the hand is correct. If you have the same stitch count on the gusset as you will later have for the hand, you can just knit in a waste yarn, place these stitches back on the left needle and knit them as if nothing had happened. If the stitch count is larger than for the hand, you have to use the cast-on method. Personally I think it is best avoided because it can be difficult to find the stitches when I need to pick them up.

SHAPING THE TOP OF THE MITTEN AND TOP OF THE THUMB

Another characteristic of the classic Norwegian mitten is the pointed tip at the top of the hand and thumb, with the dividing line between the sides following the shaping lines. It's a good idea to make the mitten hand slightly longer than the wearer's hand because mittens can shrink with wear and washing.

The decreases to shape the top are very simple. You just decrease 1 stitch on each side of the dividing line on every round (that means 4 stitches are decreased on every round). Always work the decreases with the main (background) color unless otherwise specified in the pattern instructions. Note: So that the decreases will be smooth and symmetrical, they should turn in towards the center (see close-up below & on p. 21). That means that you will decrease with different methods before and after the pattern. Before the pattern, decrease with ssk or slip 1, knit 1, pass slipped stitch over (sl 1-k1-psso). On the opposite side, knit 2 together.

Repeat the decreases on every round until 3 sts remain on the back of the hand and 3 sts on the palm. Now you can finish with a double decrease on each side: Slip 1, knit 2 together, pass slipped stitch over. End by cutting yarn and bringing it through the last 2 sts; tighten yarn and weave in tail neatly on wrong side.

In some cases, the back of the hand and the palm might not have the same number of stitches. For those mittens, begin the shaping sooner on the side with the most stitches. For example: If the back of the hand has 29 stitches and the palm 33, begin the decreases on the palm 2 rounds before beginning those for the back of the hand. That way, you'll soon have the same number of stitches and can shape each side evenly to the top of the mitten.

THUMB PATTERNS

Generally the thumb has a rather advanced pattern as for the back of the hand and that means there could be relatively many stitches. The older mittens often had a large and thick thumb but it's obvious the knitter used smaller needles. If you want a better fitting thumb, then you should also use a size or two smaller needle for the thumbs.

When the hand is knitted and the top finished, you can pick up the stitches for the thumb. Hold the mitten with palm facing you and pick up and knit the same number of stitches that you had cast on earlier over the gap. In addition pick up and knit one stitch on the side of the thumbhole. Move the stitches from the holder to the needles and work following the pattern chart; end by picking up and knitting 1 stitch from the other side of the thumbhole. It is easy to get a small hole or loose stitches on each side at the base of the thumb. Many don't like this but if you want to avoid holes, you can sew it together after the thumb is completed.

On the back of the thumb, work the same pattern as for the palm. On the finest gloves, it is not easy to determine the shift from the hand to the thumb but on most of them you can see where the knitting shifts direction. The front of the thumb has an independent composition that can be a repeat of one motif of the border around the cuff. The dividing line is most often only a dash that runs up from the gusset. The thumb tip is shaped as for the top of the mitten by decreasing with ssk and k2tog on each side of the dividing line.

Here is a little trick for smoothly and invisibly aligning the palm pattern from the hand with that on the inside of the thumb. When you cast on the new stitches, cast on matching the colors of the

stitches just below. Later, when you pick up the thumb stitches, pick up exactly the same colors as on the cast-on stitches. It will look as if you made two rounds at the same time, but, when you are finished, it will look perfect.

Don't worry if you don't get it exactly right – none of the mittens from earlier times were completely error free either!

MUTATION: THE GLOVE

Simply put, a glove is just a mitten with fingers.

Now that you are familiar with the construction of mittens, you can take the next step and knit some gloves. The cuff, thumb and hand are worked the same way as for a mitten. When you have worked up the hand to the base of the fingers, for example, after the first star (if you have chosen a typical pattern), you divide up the stitches for the fingers. In published patterns for gloves, the number of stitches for each finger is already figured out but you can use the formula below to adapt any mitten design for gloves.

Look at the pattern chart and count the stitches on the back and front of the hand. For the time

1. *Cast on the new palm stitches in the pattern as established. The best method is the backwards loop cast-on.*

2. *...pick up and knit the same colors on the back of the thumb,*

being, omit the dividing lines (the "dancing ants") at the sides. Divide the stitch count on the back of the hand and palm by 4 (for 4 fingers).

Example: If you have 31 stitches on the back and 33 on the inside of the hand, there will be 31 : 4 and 33 : 4.
31 : 4 = three fingers with 8 stitches and one with 7 on the back.

33 : 4 = three fingers with 8 stitches and one with 9 on the inside.

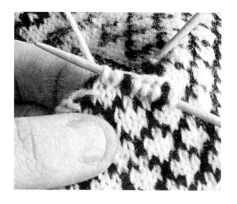

3. *... and the shift from the hand to the thumb is invisible.*

You'll note that the block pattern for the back of the hand gives you 8 stitches for the index, middle and ring fingers, and 7 stitches for the little finger.

Correspondingly, you'll see that there are 8 stitches for the index, ring, and little fingers, and 9 stitches for the middle finger. It is larger and needs some extra stitches.

Knit the fingers one after the other. In this example, we'll begin with the little finger which is also how the sequence starts in the patterns that follow.

Work the pattern for the back of the hand and palm up to the base of the little finger. Keep the stitches for the little finger on the needles and put the remaining stitches on a stitch holder or waste yarn. Place the stitches for the front of the finger on needle 1, the "dancing ants" on needle 2, and the back on the hand stitches on needle 3. With the fourth needle, cast on some extra stitches, usually 2 to 4, depending on your gauge, how big your finger is or the stitch count for the pattern. The extra stitches create a bit of knit fabric between the ring and little fingers. At the same time, you can also begin the stripe up the hand side of the little finger, opposite the "dancing ants." Arrange the needles so you can knit in the round and work following the chart. It may be necessary to increase the number of the stitches on the front of the finger to get the correct stitch count for the pattern. Work the pattern on the palm side as established. Arrange the stitches on the needles as you like best. Shape the tip of the finger as for the tip of the thumb.

Next, knit the ring finger. Begin by picking up and knitting in the extra stitches you cast on for the little finger. Align the pattern stitches so that the dividing line from the little finger flows onto the ring finger. Slip the ring finger stitches from the holder to the needles. Now cast on some extra stitches between the ring and middle fingers as you did for the little finger. Join to knit in the round and work the pattern as set. Finish with the same top shaping as for the other fingers.

The middle finger is worked as for the ring finger. Pick up and knit the stitches between the ring and middle fingers and slip the stitches from the holder to the needles, cast on extra stitches between the middle and index fingers; join to knit in the round and work following the pattern.

The index finger is worked as for the little finger but mirror image. The line along the thumb gusset flows into the dividing line for the index finger. You won't need to cast on any extra stitches for the index finger.

The knitter must decide on how long to make the fingers. On many of the older gloves, each of the fingers was knit to the same length but eventually fingers were sized for the hands of the wearer. Some gloves were fit even more precisely. It's always a good idea to make the fingers a bit long. They will shrink after being washed a few times.

The thumbs on gloves are knit just as for mittens thumbs.

YARN, KNITTING NEEDLES, GAUGE, AND SIZING

It's always possible to change the size of gloves by using a different yarn and smaller or larger needles. This is particularly appropriate for knitting small garments such as mittens and gloves.

All of the patterns in this book can be knit in any size. Because the sizes are given for an adult size with a thick 3-ply yarn, you can easily work the same pattern for a child's size by using a 2-ply

CASTING ON AND INCREASING

When the instructions tell you to cast on new stitches, it means that you should use the backwards loop cast-on method.

To increase means to make an extra stitch between two stitches by knitting into the stitch below.

1. The photo shows round 2 of the little finger. Note the dark stitch – it will form the dividing line on the inside of the finger.

2. Beginning of the ring finger. Use a crochet hook to more easily pick up and knit the extra stitches cast on for the little finger.

3. The middle finger. I've just cast on the three new stitches before joining the needles to knit in the round.

yarn and finer needles. In the same way, a child's size can be made for an adult by working with thicker yarn and bigger needles. Many glove patterns fit a woman's hand; maybe that is because women knit the gloves and tried them on for size as they knit.

DESIGNING GLOVES FOR YOUR OWN HANDS

You can experiment on your own and make gloves from a mitten pattern and vice versa. You can use any colors you like and decide on the gauge and length of fingers yourself. Combine the motifs just as you like, maybe adapting some pattern motifs from other garments. This is how the folk tradition has been kept alive and fresh for our modern needs. Traditions become lifeless when the boundaries are too tightly set and the knitting rules are too restrictive.

When I researched gloves from earlier times, I discovered something important. Even when the knitters were old and had a lot of experience, they weren't necessarily more competent or clever than us younger knitters. They followed patterns, made mistakes, fixed things later on – or let it be. The stitches might be both too tight and too loose. There might be a hole at the base of the thumb and the lines between the fingers didn't always match.

What did knitters in the past do better than us today? First and foremost they were more accepting of mistakes they made. I know knitters who rip and struggle, who unravel their knitted sweater as they sit and complain. Some toss out the yarn and needles because they can't continue unless the garment is perfect and error free.

Today we expect that everything that is made should be perfect, with a clear and obvious pattern and mistake-free finishing. Perhaps it is because we see so many mass-produced goods. When a design is prepared for industrial production, the pattern must always be suitable for the machines and the product must be free of mistakes.

Knitting is a folk hand work and not high art. It is precisely those small errors; the bits that don't quite fit that indicate a handmade item. These are the qualities that give life to the garment, as opposed to the stiffness that characterizes perfect artistry and mechanical production.

I believe that always following the rules and making everything perfectly is useless. Knitters ought to feel confident and satisfied with the work they do, and not criticize themselves because it wasn't good enough. No one is error free; our mistakes and shortcomings make us special, attractive and exciting individuals.

But all things considered – if you make a mistake that means you won't want to wear the garment, of course you should fix it. The mistake shouldn't plague you if you leave it in. In any case, you can continue along the path of Norwegian knitting traditions and make a garment with a charm that machine-produced garments will never have.

ABBREVIATIONS

BO	bind off (= British cast off)
CC	contrast color (pattern)
cm	centimeter(s)
CO	cast on
dpn	double-pointed needle(s)
g	gram(s)
gauge	= British tension
in	inch(es)
k	knit
k2tog	knit 2 together
M1	make 1 = lift strand between two stitches and knit into back loop
MC	main color (background)
mm	millimeter(s)
ndl(s)	needle(s)
p	purl
psso	pass slipped stitch over
rem	remain, remaining
rnd(s)	round(s)
RS	right side
sl	slip
ssk	(slip 1 knitwise) 2 times, insert left needle tip into front of sts and knit together
st(s)	stitch(es)
stockinette	= British stocking stitch
tbl	through back loop
WS	wrong side

GARMENT CARE—
WASHING & BLOCKING MITTENS

After knitting the mittens or gloves, finish them by gently hand washing in lukewarm water and wool safe soap. Rinse in same temperature water and then lightly squeeze (do not wring) out excess water. Roll garments in a hand towel to absorb more water, and then lay flat to dry. Make sure pieces are blocked to correct size.

PATTERNS

Lilies: Woman's Mittens

The lily is a beloved motif in the fine and decorative arts. It is the Virgin Mary's flower and, in Christian belief, the lily symbolizes pure virginal love.

SIZE: WOMAN'S
YARN: ASK HIFA 2 (SPORT, 100% WOOL, 344 YDS / 315 M, 100 G), 40 G WHITE 6047 AND 35 G GRAY 6052
NEEDLES: SET OF 4 OR 5 DPN U.S. SIZE 1.5 / 2.5 MM OR SIZE NEEDED TO OBTAIN GAUGE
GAUGE: 28 STS = 4 IN / 10 CM
STITCH COUNT: 64 STS AROUND HAND X APPROX 59 ROWS FOR LENGTH OF HAND

NOTE: To avoid long floats on the WS between color changes, twist the strand you are knitting with around the unused strand whenever there are more than 4 sts between color changes. Be careful not to pull the strand that floats.

RIGHT HAND MITTEN
With white, CO 56 sts; divide onto dpn and join, being careful not to twist cast-on row. *Work 3 rnds in k1, p1 ribbing and then knit 1 rnd with white. With gray, work 1 rnd k1, p1 ribbing and then knit 1 rnd. Work from * a total of 6 times. Finish cuff by knitting 2 rnds with white.

Now begin working charted pattern for right hand mitten. Use M1 to increase for the extra sts for the thumb gusset, knitting into the inc on the following rnd. On rnd 4, begin thumb gusset: K4, pm, M1, k3, M1, pm. On the next rnd, knit the new sts in pattern. Increase on rnds as indicated on chart until there are 13 sts for thumb gusset.
On the rnd above the red line on the chart, remove markers, place the 13 sts underlined with red onto a holder for thumb and then CO 13 new sts following the pattern on the chart (CO with backward loop method) = 64 sts around.

Annemor V766.1

Continue in charted pattern to top of mitten. Always work decreases with gray on the front of the mitten and white on the palm. Decrease on each side of the white lines up the sides of mitten. Work dec at right side of front (back) with ssk or sl 1-k1-psso; on the left side, k2tog. When 4 sts remain, cut yarn and pull tail through rem sts.

THUMB
Place the 13 sts from holder onto ndl and then, in pattern, pick up and knit 13 sts into CO row at top of thumbhole (use a crochet hook to pick up sts if necessary): 13 + 13 = 26 sts for thumb. Work following the thumb chart; on the first rnd, k2tog at each side to avoid holes and for correct stitch count: 13 + 11 = 24 sts. Work following chart to thumb shaping. If the thumb is too short at this point (it should reach middle of thumbnail), work more rounds as needed for desired thumb length. Shape top of thumb as for top of mitten.

LEFT HAND MITTEN
Work as for right hand making sure that you follow the chart for Left Hand.

FINISHING
Weave in all tails neatly on WS. See page 25 for information on garment care.

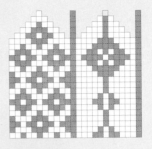

THUMB

RIGHT HAND

LEFT HAND

31

Reindeer: Child's Mittens

In old folk beliefs, both white and brown reindeer bore messages from the spirit world. By taking some color from nature you can infuse a bit of the reindeer spirit into your mittens. You can use lichens from stones to dye the pattern colors. Pick lichens four times the yarn's weight and simmer the yarn in it. After about an hour you'll have a lovely red brown color.

The food that reindeer eat, lichens, gives the yarn a light yellow shade that you can use for the background color. Simmer the lichen for an hour, strain out lichens, and then simmer the yarn in the dye bath for an hour. Wash and rinse the yarn well afterwards.

Don't forget to shake out the specks of lichen after you dye the yarn!

SIZE: CHILD'S
YARN: ASK HIFA 2 (SPORT, 100% WOOL, 344 YDS / 315 M, 100 G), 30 G GRAY 6055, 25 G BROWN 6009 (CAN BE LICHEN DYED — SEE ABOVE)
NEEDLES: SET OF 4 OR 5 DPN U.S. SIZE 2.5 / 3 MM OR SIZE NEEDED TO OBTAIN GAUGE
GAUGE: 28 STS = 4 IN / 10 CM
STITCH COUNT: 48 STS AROUND HAND X APPROX 53 ROWS FOR LENGTH OF HAND

NOTE: To avoid long floats on the WS between color changes, twist the strand you are knitting with around the unused strand whenever there are more than 4 sts between color changes. Be careful not to pull the strand that floats.

RIGHT HAND MITTEN

With gray, CO 36 sts; divide onto dpn and join, being careful not to twist cast-on row. Work 27 rnds k1tbl, p1 ribbing in the following color sequence: 7 rnds gray, 2 rnds brown, 4 rnds gray, 4 rnds brown, 4 rnds gray, 2 rnds brown, 4 rnds gray. Finish cuff by knitting 1 rnd with grey and, at the same time, increase 4 sts evenly spaced around = 40 sts. Knit 1 rnd brown.

Annemor V711.11

Now begin working charted pattern for right hand mitten. Use M1 to increase for the extra sts for the thumb gusset, knitting into the inc on the following rnd. On rnd 3, begin thumb gusset: K3, pm, M1, k1, M1, pm. On the next rnd, knit the new sts in pattern. Increase on rnds as indicated on chart until there are 13 sts for thumb gusset.

On the rnd above the red line on the chart, remove markers and place the 13 sts underlined with red onto a holder for thumb and then CO 13 new sts following the pattern on the chart (CO with backward loop method) = 48 sts around.

Continue in charted pattern to top of mitten. Always work decreases with gray. Decrease on each side of the brown lines up the sides of mitten. Work dec at right side (just after dividing line at side) of front (back) with ssk or sl 1-k1-psso; on the left side (before dividing line), k2tog. When 4 sts remain, cut yarn and pull tail through rem sts.

THUMB

Place the 13 sts from holder onto ndl and then, in pattern, pick up and knit 11 sts into CO row at top of thumbhole (use a crochet hook to pick up

sts if necessary): 13 + 11 = 24 sts for thumb. Work following the thumb chart, and, on the first rnd, k2tog at each side to avoid holes and for correct stitch count: 13 + 9 = 22 sts. Work following chart to thumb shaping. If the thumb is too short at this point (it should reach middle of thumbnail), work more rounds as needed for desired thumb length. Shape top of thumb as for top of mitten. When 6 sts rem, cut yarn and pull tail through rem sts.

LEFT HAND MITTEN

Work as for right hand making sure that you follow the chart for Left Hand.

FINISHING

Weave in all tails neatly on WS. See page 25 for information on garment care.

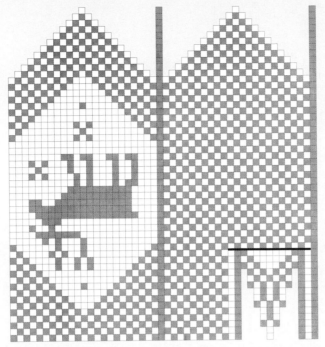

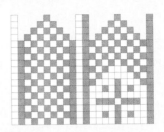

THUMB

RIGHT HAND

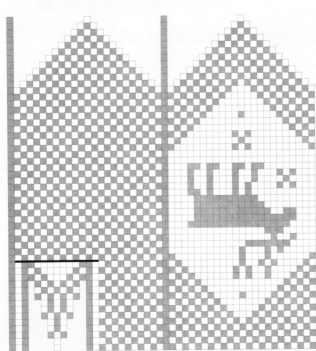

LEFT HAND

Dogs and Hearts

The dog symbolizes faithfulness and the heart love. The green color represents immortality and things that last forever. You can choose a thumb gusset with a place for a coded and confidential message. The white gusset has space for a heart that can be embroidered on later with duplicate stitch. The original mitten with 45 sts to every 4 in / 10 cm wasn't hand knitted. It has been re-designed for hand knitting and to fit an adult's hand.

SIZE: WOMAN'S
YARN: ASK HIFA 2 (SPORT, 100% WOOL, 344 YDS / 315 M, 100 G), 40 G WHITE 6047; 10 G EACH DARK ROSE RED 6015, GREEN 6026, AND BLUE 6038
NEEDLES: SET OF 4 OR 5 DPN U.S. SIZE 1.5 / 2.5 MM OR SIZE NEEDED TO OBTAIN GAUGE
GAUGE: 28 STS = 4 IN / 10 CM
STITCH COUNT: 62 STS AROUND HAND X APPROX 60 ROWS FOR LENGTH OF HAND

NOTE: To avoid long floats on the WS between color changes, twist the strand you are knitting with around the unused strand whenever there are more than 4 sts between color changes. Be careful not to pull the strand that floats.

RIGHT HAND MITTEN

With white, CO 44 sts; divide onto dpn and join, being careful not to twist cast-on row. Work in k2, p2 ribbing for approx 2_ in / 7 cm. Finish cuff by knitting 1 rnd with white, and, at the same time, increase 8 sts evenly spaced around = 52 sts. Knit 2 rnds with white.

Now begin working charted pattern for right hand mitten. The white thumb gusset allows you to add a little confidential note to the mitten and you knit

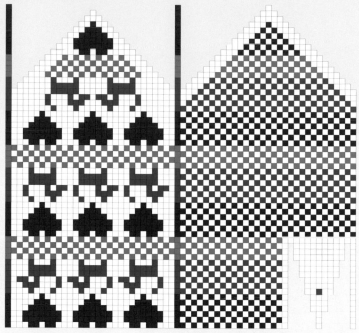

RIGHT HAND

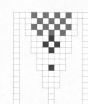

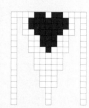

1. Knit pattern choice for thumb gusset

2. Heart sewn on with duplicate st

If you want a heart on the thumb gusset, knit the gusset with white yarn and then embroider on the heart with duplicate stitch afterwards.

LEFT HAND

Annemor V555.5

what you like for the thumb. If you want a heart on the gusset, work it entirely in white and then later embroider on the heart with duplicate stitches.

On rnd 4 of hand, begin thumb gusset: K1, pm, M1, k1, M1, pm. Use M1 to increase for the extra sts for the thumb gusset, knitting into the inc on the following rnd. Increase on rnds as indicated on chart until there are 13 sts for thumb gusset.

On the rnd above the yellow line on the chart, remove markers, place the 13 sts underlined with yellow onto a holder for thumb and then CO 13 new sts following the pattern on the chart (CO with backward loop method) = 62 sts around.

Continue in charted pattern to top of mitten. Always work decreases with white. Decrease on each side of the contrast color lines up the sides of mitten. Work dec at right side (just after dividing line at side) of front (back) with ssk or sl 1-k1-psso; on the left side (before dividing line), k2tog. When 4 sts remain, cut yarn and pull tail through rem sts.

THUMB

Place the 13 sts from holder onto ndl and then, in pattern, pick up and knit 15 sts into CO row at top of thumbhole (use a crochet hook to pick up

sts if necessary): 13 + 15 = 28 sts for thumb. Work following the thumb chart; on the first rnd, k2tog at each side to avoid holes and for correct stitch count: 13 + 13 = 26 sts. Knit the thumb with white. Measure the wearer's hand to make sure the thumb will be long enough, approx 2¾ in / 7 cm. Shape top by working around with k2tog until 4 sts rem. Cut yarn and pull tail through rem sts.

LEFT HAND MITTEN

Work as for right hand making sure that you follow the chart for Left Hand.

FINISHING

Weave in all tails neatly on WS. See page 25 for information on garment care.

39

Happy Couple

The dancing couple and lovers are full of life and happy. The three-leaf clover is often a symbol for the trinity in Christian belief but, in folk beliefs, the three-leaf clover is a sign of power and vitality because it grows so prolifically. In medieval love poems it symbolized a place for lovers' assignations.

SIZE: CHILD'S
YARN: ASK HIFA 2 (SPORT, 100% WOOL, 344 YDS / 315 M, 100 G), 25 G DARK ROSE RED 6015; 15 G WHITE 6047
NEEDLES: SET OF 4 OR 5 DPN U.S. SIZE 1.5 / 2.5 MM OR SIZE NEEDED TO OBTAIN GAUGE
GAUGE: 28 STS = 4 IN / 10 CM
STITCH COUNT: 54 STS AROUND HAND X APPROX 42 ROWS FOR LENGTH OF HAND

NOTE: To avoid long floats on the WS between color changes, twist the strand you are knitting with around the unused strand whenever there are more than 4 sts between color changes. Be careful not to pull the strand that floats.

RIGHT HAND MITTEN
With red, CO 38 sts; divide onto dpn and join, being careful not to twist cast-on row. Work 17 rnds in k1, p1 ribbing in the following color sequence: 6 rnds red, 1 rnd white, 1 rnd red, 1 rnd white, 1 rnd red, 1 rnd white, 6 rnds red. Finish cuff by knitting 1 rnd with red and, at the same time, increase 8 sts evenly spaced around = 46 sts.

Now begin working charted pattern for right hand mitten. On rnd 6 of hand, begin thumb gusset: K4, pm, M1, k1, M1, pm. Use M1 to increase for the extra sts for the thumb gusset, knitting into the inc on the following rnd. Increase on rnds as indicated on chart until there are 13 sts for thumb gusset.
On the rnd above the red line on the chart, remove markers, place the 13 sts underlined with red onto a holder for thumb and then CO 13 new sts following the pattern on the chart (CO with backward loop method) = 54 sts around.

Annemor V714.4

Continue in charted pattern to top of mitten. Try on mitten to make sure it will be long enough—it should reach the top of the little finger. If necessary work a few more rounds before shaping. Always work decreases with red. Decrease on each side of the contrast color lines up the sides of mitten. Work dec at right side (just after dividing line at side) of front (back) with ssk or sl 1-k1-psso; on the left side (before dividing line), k2tog. When 6 sts remain, cut yarn and pull tail through rem sts.

THUMB

Place the 13 sts from holder onto ndl and then, in pattern, pick up and knit 13 sts into CO row at top of thumbhole (use a crochet hook to pick up sts if necessary): 13 + 13 = 26 sts for thumb. Work following the thumb chart; on the first rnd, k2tog at each side to avoid holes and for correct stitch count: 13 + 11 = 24 sts. Try on mitten to make sure thumb is long enough – it should reach to middle of thumbnail. If necessary, work a few more rounds before shaping top. Shape top of thumb as for top of mitten. When 4 sts remain, cut yarn and pull tail through rem sts.

LEFT HAND MITTEN

Work as for right hand making sure that you follow the chart for Left Hand.

FINISHING

Weave in all tails neatly on WS. See page 25 for information on garment care.

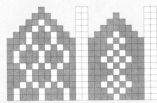

THUMB

RIGHT HAND

LEFT HAND

Reassurance Mittens

Going "hand in hand" signifies security and friendship. A handshake is a friendly greeting with anyone you meet along the way. The knitter of the original mittens didn't use the same red yarn on the ribbing of the right and left hands, so, you can choose light or deep red or maybe you want a totally different color for your pair of mittens.

SIZE: CHILD'S
YARN: ASK HIFA 2 (SPORT, 100% WOOL, 344 YDS / 315 M, 100 G), 20 G WHITE 6047; 13 G EACH BLACK 6053 AND RED 6014
NEEDLES: SET OF 4 OR 5 DPN U.S. SIZE 2.5 / 3 MM FOR CHILD'S SIZE; U.S. 1.5 / 2.5 MM FOR BABY SIZE OR SIZE NEEDED TO OBTAIN GAUGE
GAUGE: U.S. 2.5 / 3 MM: 24 STS = 4 IN /10 CM; U.S. 1.5 / 2.5 MM: 28 STS = 4 IN / 10 CM
STITCH COUNT: 42 STS AROUND HAND X APPROX 41 ROWS FOR LENGTH OF HAND

NOTE: To avoid long floats on the WS between color changes, twist the strand you are knitting with around the unused strand whenever there are more than 4 sts between color changes. Be careful not to pull the strand that floats.

RIGHT HAND MITTEN
With red, CO 36 sts; divide onto dpn and join, being careful not to twist cast-on row. Work in k1,

p1 ribbing in the following color sequence: 8 rnds red, 2 rnds white, 2 rnds black, 2 rnds white, 8 rnds red for a total of 22 rnds. Finish cuff by knitting 1 rnd with red, and, at the same time, increase 2 sts evenly spaced around = 38 sts.

Now begin working charted pattern for right hand mitten. On rnd 7 of hand, begin thumb gusset: K1, pm, M1, k3, M1, pm. Use M1 to increase for the extra sts for the thumb gusset, knitting into the inc on the following rnd. Increase on rnds as indicated on chart until there are 9 sts for thumb gusset.
On the rnd above the red line on the chart, remove markers, place the 9 sts underlined with red onto a holder for thumb and then CO 9 new sts following the pattern on the chart (CO with backward loop method) = 42 sts around.

Continue in charted pattern to top of mitten. Try on mitten to make sure it will be long enough – it should reach the top of the little finger. If neces-

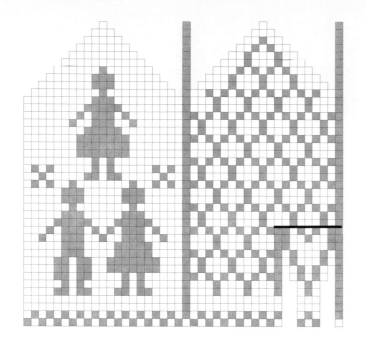

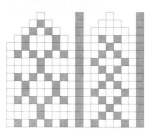

THUMB

RIGHT HAND

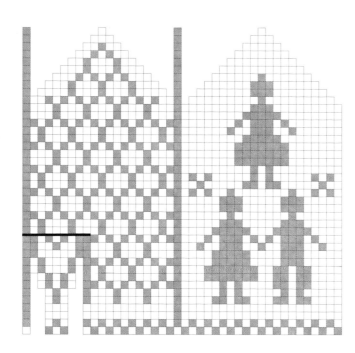

LEFT HAND

sary work a few more rounds before shaping. Al-ways work decreases with white. Decrease on each side of the contrast color lines up the sides of mit-ten. Work dec at right side (just after dividing line at side) of front (back) with ssk or sl 1-k1-psso; on the left side (before dividing line), k2tog. When 4 sts remain, cut yarn and pull tail through rem sts.

THUMB
Place the 9 sts from holder onto ndl and then, in pattern, pick up and knit 11 sts into CO row at top of thumbhole (use a crochet hook to pick up sts if necessary): 9 + 11 = 20 sts for thumb. Work following the thumb chart; on the first rnd, k2tog at each side to avoid holes and for correct stitch count: 9 + 9 = 18 sts. Try on mitten to make sure thumb is long enough – it should reach to middle of thumbnail. If necessary, work a few more rounds before shaping top. Shape top of thumb as for top of mitten. Cut yarn and pull tail through rem sts.

LEFT HAND MITTEN
Work as for right hand making sure that you follow the chart for Left Hand.

FINISHING
Weave in all tails neatly on WS. See page 25 for information on garment care.

Annemor V713

47

Bird in the Window

You can easily dye the yarn for these bird mittens yourself. For the pattern color, simmer the yarn in a dye bath with lichens for an hour. For the strongest color, use an amount of lichens four times the weight of the yarn. If you strain out the lichens and simmer the wool in the dye bath for an hour, you'll get a nice background color.

SIZE: CHILD'S
YARN: ASK HIFA 2 (SPORT, 100% WOOL, 344 YDS / 315 M, 100 G), 26 G BRASS 6092; 14 G HEATHERY DARK BROWN 6103 (IF DESIRED, A SMALL AMOUNT OF WHITE FOR THE CUFF STRIPES AS ON ORIGINAL PAIR)
NEEDLES: SET OF 4 OR 5 DPN U.S. SIZE 2.5 / 3 MM FOR CHILD'S SIZE AND U.S. 1.5 / 2.5 MM FOR BABY SIZE OR SIZE NEEDED TO OBTAIN GAUGE
GAUGE: U.S. 2.5 / 3 MM: 24 STS = 4 IN /10 CM; U.S. 1.5 / 2.5 MM: 28 STS = 4 IN / 10 CM
STITCH COUNT: 46 STS AROUND HAND X APPROX 42 ROWS FOR LENGTH OF HAND

NOTE: To avoid long floats on the WS between color changes, twist the strand you are knitting with around the unused strand whenever there are more than 4 sts between color changes. Be careful not to pull the strand that floats.

RIGHT HAND MITTEN

With brass, CO 36 sts; divide onto dpn and join, being careful not to twist cast-on row. Work in k1 tbl, p1 ribbing in the following color sequence: 10 rnds brass, 2 rnds brown, 6 rnds brass, 2 rnds brown, 8 rnds brass for a total of 28 rnds. Finish cuff by knitting 1 rnd with brass, and, at the same time, increase 6 sts evenly spaced around = 42 sts.

Now begin working charted pattern for right hand mitten. On rnd 4 of hand, begin thumb gusset: K2, pm, M1, k3, M1, pm. Use M1 to increase for the extra sts for the thumb gusset, knitting into the inc on the following rnd. Increase on rnds as indicated on chart until there are 9 sts for thumb gusset.
On the rnd above the red line on the chart, remove markers, place the 9 sts underlined with red onto a holder for thumb and then CO 9 new sts following the pattern on the chart (CO with backward loop method) = 46 sts around.

Annemor V711.1

Continue in charted pattern to top of mitten. Try on mitten to make sure it will be long enough – it should reach the top of the little finger. If necessary work a few more rounds before shaping. Always work decreases with brass. Decrease on each side of the contrast color lines up the sides of mitten. Work dec at right side (just after dividing line at side) of front (back) with ssk or sl 1-k1-psso; on the left side (before dividing line), k2tog. When 6 sts remain, cut yarn and pull tail through rem sts.

THUMB
Place the 9 sts from holder onto ndl and then, in pattern, pick up and knit 13 sts into CO row at top of thumbhole (use a crochet hook to pick up sts if necessary): 9 + 13 = 22 sts for thumb. Work following the thumb chart; on the first rnd, k2tog at each side to avoid holes and for correct stitch count: 9 + 11 = 20 sts. Try on mitten to make sure thumb is long enough – it should reach to middle of thumbnail. If necessary, work a few more rounds before shaping top. Shape top of thumb as for top of mitten. When 4 sts rem, cut yarn and pull tail through rem sts.

LEFT HAND MITTEN
Work as for right hand making sure that you follow the chart for Left Hand.

FINISHING
Weave in all tails neatly on WS. See page 25 for information on garment care.

THUMB

RIGHT HAND

LEFT HAND

The Moose and the World's Tree

In Norn mythology, the world's tree, "Yggdrasil," is an ash tree with its crown reaching into the heavens and its roots in the underworld. The myth relates that the first man, the forefather of everyone on earth, was created from the trunk of this ash tree. (As a coincidence, the yarn for these mittens is named Ask (ash) Hifa 2). The moose, deer, and reindeer are symbols of piety and religious longing, as in this biblical quote from Psalms 42 "As the deer thirsts for running water, my soul thirsts for you, my Lord.

SIZE: WOMAN'S/ MAN'S

YARN: ASK HIFA 2 (SPORT, 100% WOOL, 344 YDS / 315 M, 100 G), 60 G LIGHT HEATHER BROWN 6058 AND 35 G RED 6014

NEEDLES: SET OF 4 OR 5 DPN U.S. SIZE 1.5 / 2.5 MM OR SIZE NEEDED TO OBTAIN GAUGE

GAUGE: 28 STS = 4 IN / 10 CM

STITCH COUNT: 71 STS AROUND HAND X APPROX 68 ROWS FOR LENGTH OF HAND

SIZING NOTE: LARGER SIZE MITTENS CAN BE KNIT WITH HIFA 3 YARN AND NEEDLES U.S. 2.5 OR 4 / 3 OR 3.5 MM.

NOTE: To avoid long floats on the WS between color changes, twist the strand you are knitting with around the unused strand whenever there are more than 4 sts between color changes. Be careful not to pull the strand that floats.

RIGHT HAND MITTEN

With light brown, CO 52 sts; divide onto dpn and join, being careful not to twist cast-on row. Work in k2, p2 ribbing in the following color sequence: 12 rnds light brown, 4 rnds red, 4 rnds light brown, 4 rnds red, 12 rnds light brown for a total of 36 rnds. Next, with light brown, increasing 13 sts evenly spaced around on the first rnd, knit 3 rnds, = 65 sts.

Now begin working charted pattern for right hand mitten. Use M1 to increase for the extra sts for the thumb gusset, knitting into the inc on the following rnd. On rnd 4, begin thumb gusset: k3 pm, M1, k5, M1, pm. On the next rnd, knit the new sts in pattern. Increase on rnds as indicated on chart until there are 17 sts for thumb gusset.
On the rnd above the red line on the chart, remove

Annemor V711.12

markers, place the 17 sts underlined with red onto a holder for thumb and then CO 17 new sts following the pattern on the chart (CO with backward loop method) = 71 sts around.

Continue in charted pattern to top of mitten. The length of the mitten can be adjusted for either a woman's or man's size. Have the person who will wear the mitten try it on to make sure it fits. Always work decreases with light brown. Decrease on each side of the contrast color lines up the sides of mitten. Work dec at right side of front (back) with ssk or sl 1-k1-psso; on the left side, k2tog. When 8 sts remain, cut yarn and pull tail through rem sts.

THUMB

Place the 17 sts from holder onto ndl and then, in pattern, pick up and knit 15 sts into CO row at top of thumbhole (use a crochet hook to pick up sts if necessary): 17 + 15 = 32 sts for thumb. Work following the thumb chart; on the first rnd, k2tog at each side to avoid holes and for correct stitch count: 17 + 13 = 30 sts. Work following chart to thumb shaping. If the thumb is too short at this point (it should reach middle of thumbnail), work more rounds as needed for desired thumb length. Shape top of thumb as for top of mitten.

LEFT HAND MITTEN

Work as for right hand making sure that you follow the chart for Left Hand.

FINISHING

Weave in all tails neatly on WS. See page 25 for information on garment care.

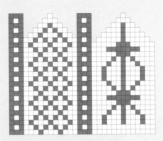

THUMB

RIGHT HAND

LEFT HAND

The King of the Woods

The moose is the king of the woods. He is one of the most common animals and has become an important tourist attraction as well as a favorite motif on souvenirs. The knitter of the original gloves put the thumb on the wrong side. It was cut off and then badly sewn on in the correct place. Be careful to place the animals so that their heads meet when you have the gloves on your hands.

SIZE: WOMAN'S/MAN'S

YARN: ASK HIFA 2 (SPORT, 100% WOOL, 344 YDS / 315 M, 100 G), 60 G WHITE 6057, 40 G RED 6014, AND 15 G NAVY BLUE 6038 OR 6039

NEEDLES: SET OF 4 OR 5 DPN U.S. SIZE 1.5 / 2.5 MM OR SIZE NEEDED TO OBTAIN GAUGE

GAUGE: 28 STS = 4 IN / 10 CM

STITCH COUNT: 64 STS AROUND HAND

NOTE: To avoid long floats on the WS between color changes, twist the strand you are knitting with around the unused strand whenever there are more than 4 sts between color changes. Be careful not to pull the strand that floats.

RIGHT HAND GLOVE

With white, CO 48 sts; divide onto dpn and join, being careful not to twist cast-on row. Work 29 rnds of k2, p2 ribbing in the following color sequence: 10 rnds white, 2 rnds red, 2 rnds white, 1 rnd blue, 1 rnd white, 1 rnd blue, 1 rnd white, 1 rnd blue, 2 rnds white, 2 rnds red, 6 rnds white. Finish cuff by knitting 2 rnds with white and then working the blue and white border pattern. Now work 3 rnds white, increasing 16 sts evenly spaced around on the second rnd to 64 sts total.

Now begin working charted pattern for right hand glove. On the rnd above the red line on the chart, place the 12 sts underlined with red onto a holder for thumb and then CO 12 new sts following the pattern on the chart (CO with backward loop method) = 64 sts around.

Continue in charted pattern to the base of the fingers. Place hand sts on a holder while you knit the thumb.

THUMB

Place the 12 sts from holder onto ndl and then, with white, pick up and knit 14 sts into CO row at top of thumbhole (use a crochet hook to pick

Annemor V711.17

up sts if necessary): 12 + 14 = 26 sts for thumb. Knit the thumb with white only, and, on the first rnd, k2tog at each side to avoid holes and for correct stitch count: 12 + 12 = 24 sts. Work around in stockinette to thumb shaping. Try on the glove to make sure the thumb is long enough (it should reach middle of thumbnail); work more rounds as needed for desired thumb length. Shape top of thumb as follows: decrease at right side of front (back) with ssk or sl 1-k1-psso; on the left side, k2tog. Decrease on every round until 2-4 sts remain; cut yarn and pull through remaining sts.

INDEX FINGER
Place 9 sts from the back of the hand + 1 side st + 7 sts from palm onto ndls and CO 3 sts with backwards loop method at base of middle finger = 20 sts total. Knit around in stockinette until finger is about 2½ in / 6 cm long or desired length and then shape top as for thumb.

MIDDLE FINGER
Place 8 sts from the back of the hand onto dpn, pick up and knit 3 sts from cast-on at base of index finger, place 8 sts from palm onto ndl, and CO 3 sts with backwards loop method at base of ring finger = 22 sts total. Knit around in stockinette until finger is about 3¼ in / 8 cm long or desired length and then shape top as for thumb.

RING FINGER
Place 8 sts from the back of the hand onto dpn, pick up and knit 3 sts from cast-on at base of middle finger, place 8 sts from palm onto ndl, and CO 3 sts with backwards loop method at base of little finger = 22 sts total. Knit around in stockinette until finger is about 2¾ in / 7 cm long or desired length and then shape top as for thumb.

LITTLE FINGER
Place rem sts = 6 from back of hand + 1 side st + 8 sts from palm and then pick up and knit 3 sts along cast-on at base of ring finger = total of 18 sts. Knit around in stockinette until finger is about 2 in / 5 cm long or desired length and then shape top as for thumb.

LEFT HAND GLOVE
Work as for right hand making sure that you follow the chart for Left Hand and place thumb and fingers correctly.

FINISHING
Weave in all tails neatly on WS. See page 25 for information on garment care.

58

**BORDER PATTERN
ABOVE CUFF**

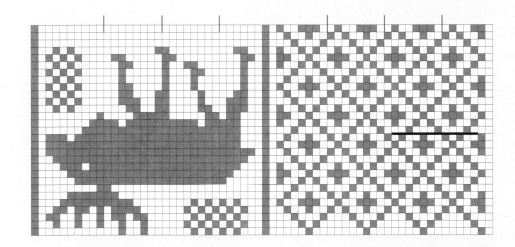

RIGHT HAND

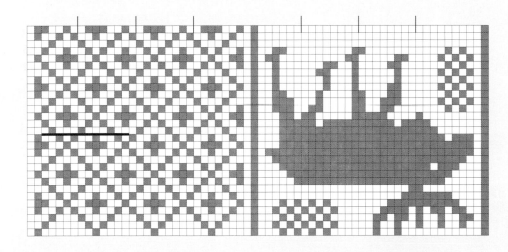

LEFT HAND

Multicolor Bird Mittens

Birds are wing-borne souls. Various bird breeds have different roles in folk beliefs.
Because birds can fly high, they can deliver messages to the heavenly gods.
The original mittens were machine-knit at a fine gauge. I've reworked the pattern
for hand knitting.

SIZE: ADULT MEDIUM
YARN: ASK HIFA 2 (SPORT, 100% WOOL, 344 YDS /
315 M, 100 G), 50 G WHITE 6057, 20 G EACH
RED 6071 AND COBALT BLUE 6039, 15 G LIGHT
BLUE 6081
NEEDLES: SET OF 4 OR 5 DPN U.S. SIZE 1.5 /
2.5 MM OR SIZE NEEDED TO OBTAIN GAUGE
GAUGE: 28 STS = 4 IN / 10 CM
STITCH COUNT: 57 STS AROUND HAND X APPROX 55
ROWS FOR LENGTH OF HAND

Annemor V523

NOTE: To avoid long floats on the WS between
color changes, twist the strand you are knitting
with around the unused strand whenever there are
more than 4 sts between color changes. Be careful
not to pull the strand that floats.

RIGHT HAND MITTEN

With white CO 48 sts. Divide sts onto dpn and join,
being careful not to twist cast-on row. If desired,
cast on with light blue, join, knit 1 rnd, and then
change to white for ribbing. Work in k2, p2 ribbing
for approx 2¾ in / 7 cm. Next, with white, and
increasing 9 sts evenly spaced around on the first
rnd knit 4 rnds = 58 sts.

RIGHT HAND

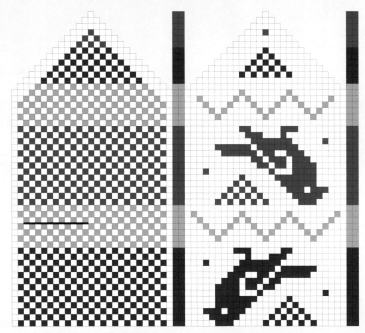

LEFT HAND

Now begin working charted pattern for right hand mitten. On the rnd above the black line on the chart, place the 11 sts underlined with black onto a holder for thumb and then CO 11 new sts following the pattern on the chart (CO with backward loop method) = 57 sts around. Instead of placing sts on a holder, you can knit across the 11 sts with smooth waste yarn, place those sts back on left needle, and knit in pattern.

Continue in charted pattern to top of mitten. Always work decreases with white. Decrease on each side of the contrast color lines up the sides of mitten. Work dec at right side of front (back) with ssk or sl 1-k1-psso; on the left side, k2tog. When 6 sts remain, cut yarn and pull tail through rem sts.

THUMB

Place the 11 sts from holder onto ndl (or remove waste yarn and place sts around thumbhole on needle) and then, with white, pick up and knit 13 sts into CO row at top of thumbhole (use a crochet hook to pick up sts if necessary): 11 + 13 = 24 sts for thumb. With white only, knit around in stockinette; on the first rnd, k2tog at each side to avoid holes and for correct stitch count: 11 + 11 = 22 sts. Work until thumb is about 2 in / 5 cm long or desired length. Shape top of thumb by working k2tog around until 4 sts rem. Cut yarn and pull tail through rem sts.

LEFT HAND MITTEN

Work as for right hand making sure that you follow the chart for Left Hand.

FINISHING

Weave in all tails neatly on WS. See page 25 for information on garment care.

The Young Maiden and Her Dream

A white reindeer might bring messages about love and can communicate through various means, especially dreams. The reindeer represents purity and renewal and, in some cultures, symbolizes virgins and young maidens. The white reindeer comes from the sun and its antlers represent sun rays and power.

SIZE: ADULT, MEDIUM
YARN: ASK HIFA 2 (SPORT, 100% WOOL, 344 YDS / 315 M, 100 G), 60 G MEDIUM BLUE 6035, 35 G WHITE 6057
NEEDLES: SET OF 4 OR 5 DPN U.S. SIZE 1.5 / 2.5 MM FOR HAND AND U.S. SIZE 0 / 2 MM FOR FINGERS OR SIZES NEEDED TO OBTAIN GAUGE
GAUGE: 28 STS ON LARGER NEEDLES = 4 IN / 10 CM
STITCH COUNT: 63 STS AROUND HAND

NOTE: To avoid long floats on the WS between color changes, twist the strand you are knitting with around the unused strand whenever there are more than 4 sts between color changes. Be careful not to pull the strand that floats.

RIGHT HAND GLOVE

With medium blue, CO 52 sts; divide onto dpn and join, being careful not to twist cast-on row. Work 27 rnds of k2, p2 ribbing in the following color sequence: 12 rnds blue, 5 rnds white, 10 rnds blue.

Finish cuff by knitting 1 rnd with blue, increasing 4 sts evenly spaced around to 56 sts. Next work the charted border pattern followed by 2 rnds with blue; on last rnd, inc 1 st = 57 sts total.

Now begin working charted pattern for right hand glove. Use M1 to increase for the extra sts for the thumb gusset, knitting into the inc on the following rnd. On rnd 3, begin thumb gusset: k4 pm, M1, k1, M1, pm. On the next rnd, knit the new sts in pattern. Increase on rnds as indicated on chart until there are 14 sts for thumb gusset.
On the rnd above the red line on the chart, remove markers, place the 14 sts underlined with red onto a holder for thumb and then CO 12 new sts following the pattern on the chart (CO with backward loop method) = 63 sts around.

Continue in charted pattern to the base of the fingers. Place hand sts on a holder while you knit the

LITTLE FINGER

MIDDLE FINGER

INDEX AND RING FINGERS

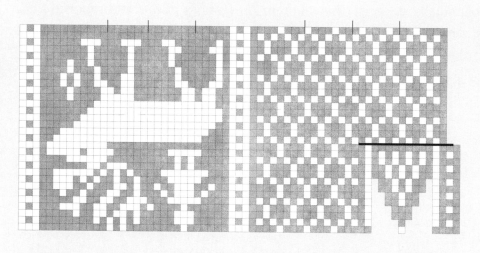

THUMB

RIGHT HAND GLOVE

**PATTERN BORDER
ABOVE CUFF**

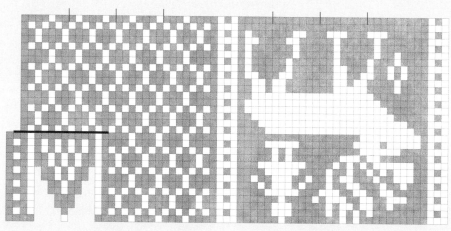

LEFT HAND GLOVE

thumb. Use a needle 1 U.S. size / 0.5 mm smaller than for hand.

THUMB

Place the 14 sts from holder onto ndl and then, with blue, pick up and knit 12 sts into CO row at top of thumbhole (use a crochet hook to pick up sts if necessary): 14 + 12 = 26 sts for thumb. Knit the thumb following charted pattern and, on the first rnd, k2tog at each side to avoid holes and for correct stitch count: 14 + 10 = 24 sts. Work following chart to thumb shaping. Try on the glove to make sure the thumb is long enough (it should reach middle of thumbnail); work more rounds as needed for desired thumb length. Shape top of thumb as follows: decrease at right side of front (back) with ssk or sl 1-k1-psso; on the left side, k2tog. When 8 sts rem, cut yarn and pull tail through rem sts.

INDEX FINGER

Place 9 sts from the back of the hand + 3 side sts + 7 sts from palm onto ndls and CO 5 sts with backwards loop method at base of middle finger = 24 sts total. Knit following chart for index finger until finger is desired length and then shape top as for thumb.

MIDDLE FINGER

Place 7 sts from the back of the hand onto dpn, pick up and knit 5 sts from cast-on at base of index finger, place 7 sts from palm onto ndl, and CO 5 sts with backwards loop method at base of ring finger = 24 sts total. Knit following chart for middle finger until finger is desired length and then shape top as for thumb.

RING FINGER

Place 7 sts from the back of the hand onto dpn, pick up and knit 5 sts from cast-on at base of middle finger, place 7 sts from palm onto ndl, and CO 5 sts with backwards loop method at base of little finger = 24 sts total. Knit following chart for ring finger until finger is desired length and then shape top as for thumb.

LITTLE FINGER

Place rem sts = 5 from back of hand + 3 side sts + 8 sts from palm and then pick up and knit 6 sts along cast-on at base of ring finger = total of 22 sts. Knit following chart for little finger until finger is about 2 in / 5 cm long or desired length and the shape top as for thumb.

LEFT HAND GLOVE

Work as for right hand making sure that you follow the chart for Left Hand and place thumb and fingers correctly.

FINISHING

Weave in all tails neatly on WS. See page 25 for information on garment care.

Annemor V711.19

Elkhound Gloves

The elkhound and "buhund" (a Norwegian type of farm dog) are completely Norwegian animals, but if we go to Finland, the same motif is called a Lapp dog. The chain border on the cuffs embodies eternal faithfulness but the other border on the cuff and fingers is called a "spit blob" in the Setesdal knitting tradition. Maybe the expression was connected with the sound of spitting, something like, "phew phew." Spitting three times was a way to wish someone prosperity and luck.

SIZE: MAN'S
YARN: ASK HIFA 2 (SPORT, 100% WOOL, 344 YDS / 315 M, 100 G), 60 G BLUE 6035, 35 G BLACK 6053
NEEDLES: SET OF 4 OR 5 DPN U.S. SIZE 1.5 OR 2.5 / 2.5 OR 3 MM OR SIZE NEEDED TO OBTAIN GAUGE
GAUGE: 28 STS = 4 IN / 10 CM
STITCH COUNT: 72 STS AROUND HAND

NOTE: To avoid long floats on the WS between color changes, twist the strand you are knitting with around the unused strand whenever there are more than 4 sts between color changes. Be careful not to pull the strand that floats.

RIGHT HAND GLOVE

With blue, CO 56 sts; divide onto dpn and join, being careful not to twist cast-on row. Work in k1, p1 ribbing for 2 rounds. Next, knit 3 rnds or work 3 more rnds ribbing. Add black and work charted cuff pattern. Finish cuff by knitting 1 rnd with blue, increasing 6 sts evenly spaced around to 62 sts. Knit 2 more rnds with blue.

Now begin working charted pattern for right hand glove. Use M1 to increase for the extra sts for the thumb gusset, knitting into the inc on the following rnd. On rnd 2, begin thumb gusset: k2, pm, M1, k1, M1, pm. On the next rnd, knit the new sts in pattern. Increase on rnds as indicated on chart until there are 15 sts for thumb gusset.
On the rnd above the red line on the chart, remove markers, place the 15 sts underlined with red onto a holder for thumb and then CO 15 new sts following the pattern on the chart (CO with backward loop method) = 72 sts around.

Continue in charted pattern to the base of the fingers. Place hand sts on a holder while you knit the thumb.

Annemor V711.2

THUMB
Place the 15 sts from holder onto ndl and then, in pattern, pick up and knit 15 sts into CO row at top of thumbhole (use a crochet hook to pick up sts if necessary): 15 + 15 = 30 sts for thumb. Work following charted pattern for thumb, and, on the first rnd, k2tog at each side to avoid holes and for correct stitch count: 15 + 13 = 28 sts. Work to thumb shaping. Try on the glove to make sure the thumb is long enough (it should reach middle of thumbnail); work more rounds as needed for desired thumb length. Shape top of thumb as follows: decrease at right side of front (back) with ssk or sl 1-k1-psso; on the left side, k2tog. When 4 sts rem, cut yarn and pull tail through rem sts.

INDEX FINGER
Place 11 sts from the back of the hand + 2 side sts + 8 sts from palm onto ndls and CO 5 sts with backwards loop method at base of middle finger = 26 sts total. Knit following chart for index finger until finger is desired length and then shape top as for thumb.

MIDDLE FINGER
Place 8 sts from the back of the hand onto dpn, pick up and knit 5 sts from cast-on at base of index finger, place 8 sts from palm onto ndl, and CO 5 sts with backwards loop method at base of ring finger = 26 sts total. Knit following chart for middle finger until finger is desired length and then shape top as for thumb.

RING FINGER
Place 8 sts from the back of the hand onto dpn, pick up and knit 5 sts from cast-on at base of middle finger, place 8 sts from palm onto ndl, and CO 5 sts with backwards loop method at base of little finger = 26 sts total. Knit following chart for ring finger until finger is desired length and then shape top as for thumb.

LITTLE FINGER
Place rem sts = 6 from back of hand + 2 side sts + 11 sts from palm and then pick up and knit 5 sts along cast-on at base of ring finger = total of 24 sts. Knit following chart for little finger until finger is about 2 in / 5 cm long or desired length and the shape top as for thumb.

LEFT HAND GLOVE
Work as for right hand making sure that you follow the chart for Left Hand and place thumb and fingers correctly.

FINISHING
Weave in all tails neatly on WS. See page 25 for information on garment care.

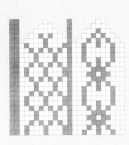
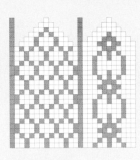

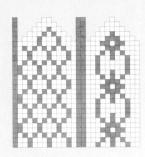

LITTLE FINGER   **RING FINGER**   **MIDDLE FINGER**   **INDEX FINGER**

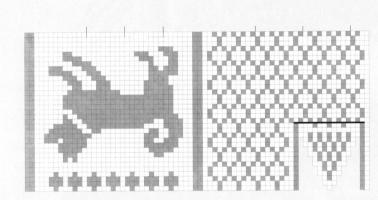
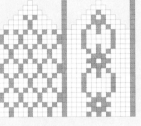

THUMB

RIGHT HAND GLOVE

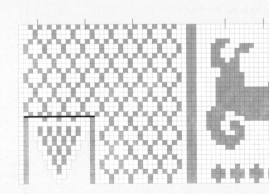
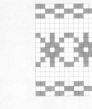

CUFF

LEFT HAND GLOVE

Wandering Reindeer

Mary Thomas' Knitting Book, published in London in 1938, shows a pair of gloves with the same color arrangements as these. The author states that the pair was from Lithuania. The gloves in the Thomas book feature the same motifs as my young maiden and reindeer glove on page 65.

SIZE: MAN'S
YARN: ASK HIFA 2 (SPORT, 100% WOOL, 344 YDS / 315 M, 100 G), 60 G NAVY BLUE 6038, 15 G CLEAR, PURE RED 6014, 30 G WHITE 6057
NEEDLES: SET OF 4 OR 5 DPN U.S. SIZE 0 / 2 MM OR SIZE NEEDED TO OBTAIN GAUGE (USE FINER YARN IF NECESSARY FOR CORRECT GAUGE)
GAUGE: 29 STS = 4 IN / 10 CM
STITCH COUNT: 76 STS AROUND HAND

NOTE: To avoid long floats on the WS between color changes, twist the strand you are knitting with around the unused strand whenever there are more than 4 sts between color changes. Be careful not to pull the strand that floats.

RIGHT HAND GLOVE
With navy blue, CO 60 sts; divide onto dpn and join, being careful not to twist cast-on row. Work in k1, p1 ribbing for 4 rounds and then knit 1 rnd. Add white and work charted cuff pattern. Finish cuff by knitting 2 rnds with blue, and then, on the 3rd rnd, increase 6 sts evenly spaced around to 68 sts. Knit 1 more rnd with blue and then work charted pattern for hand.

Now begin working charted pattern for right hand glove. Use M1 to increase for the extra sts for the thumb gusset, knitting into the inc on the following rnd. On rnd 3, begin thumb gusset: k5, pm, M1, k3, M1, pm. On the next rnd, knit the new sts in pattern. Increase on rnds as indicated on chart until there are 15 sts for thumb gusset.
On the rnd above the red line on the chart, remove markers, place the 15 sts underlined with red onto a holder for thumb and then CO 13 new sts following the pattern on the chart (CO with backward loop method) = 76 sts around.

Continue in charted pattern to the base of the fingers. Place hand sts on a holder while you knit the thumb.

THUMB

Place the 15 sts from holder onto ndl and then, in pattern, pick up and knit 15 sts into CO row at top of thumbhole (use a crochet hook to pick up sts if necessary): 15 + 15 = 30 sts for thumb. Work following charted pattern for thumb, and, on the first rnd, k2tog at each side to avoid holes and for correct stitch count: 15 + 13 = 28 sts. Work to thumb shaping. Try on the glove to make sure the thumb is long enough (it should reach middle of thumbnail); work more rounds as needed for desired thumb length. Shape top of thumb as follows: decrease at right side of front (back) with ssk or sl 1-k1-psso; on the left side, k2tog. When 4 sts rem, cut yarn and pull tail through rem sts.

INDEX FINGER

Place 11 sts from the back of the hand + 1 side st + 10 sts from palm onto ndls and CO 4 sts with backwards loop method at base of middle finger = 26 sts total. Knit following chart for index finger until finger is desired length and then shape top as for thumb.

MIDDLE FINGER

Place 8 sts from the back of the hand onto dpn, pick up and knit 4 sts from cast-on at base of index finger, place 10 sts from palm onto ndl, and CO 4 sts with backwards loop method at base of ring finger = 26 sts total. Knit following chart for middle finger until finger is desired length and then shape top as for thumb.

RING FINGER

Place 8 sts from the back of the hand onto dpn, pick up and knit 4 sts from cast-on at base of middle finger, place 10 sts from palm onto ndl, and CO 4 sts with backwards loop method at base of little finger = 26 sts total. Knit following chart for ring finger until finger is desired length and then shape top as for thumb.

LITTLE FINGER

Place rem sts = 8 from back of hand + 1 side st + 9 sts from palm and then pick up and knit 6 sts along cast-on at base of ring finger = total of 24 sts. Knit following chart for little finger until finger is about 2 in / 5 cm long or desired length and the shape top as for thumb.

LEFT HAND GLOVE

Work as for right hand making sure that you follow the chart for Left Hand and place thumb and fingers correctly.

FINISHING

Weave in all tails neatly on WS. See page 25 for information on garment care.

Annemor V711.4

74

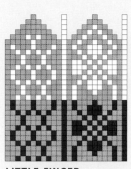 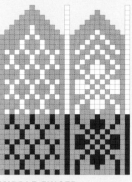 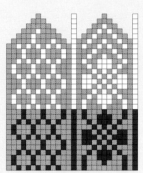

LITTLE FINGER   **MIDDLE FINGER**   **INDEX AND RING FINGERS**

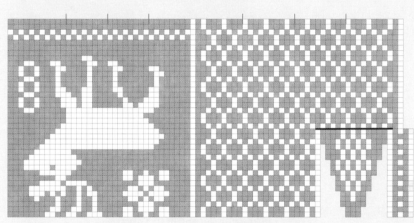

THUMB

RIGHT HAND GLOVE

CUFF

LEFT HAND GLOVE

Phoenix

I associate this pattern with the Asian motif of the firebird fighting a dragon.
The mittens were designed by Elsa Poulsson who wrote *Charts for Knitting and Embroidery*. Many of the motifs in her book were originally on knitted garments,
including mittens and gloves.

SIZE: WOMAN'S AND MAN'S
YARN: ASK HIFA 2 (SPORT, 100% WOOL, 344 YDS / 315 M, 100 G), 35 G WHITE 6057, 20 G BLACK 6053
NEEDLES: SET OF 4 OR 5 DPN U.S. SIZE 1.5 / 2.5 MM OR SIZE NEEDED TO OBTAIN GAUGE
GAUGE: 28 STS = 4 IN / 10 CM
STITCH COUNT: 61 STS AROUND HAND X APPROX 58 ROWS FOR LENGTH OF HAND
SIZING NOTE: LARGER SIZE MITTENS CAN BE KNIT WITH HIFA 3 YARN AND NEEDLES U.S. 2.5 OR 4 / 3 OR 3.5 MM.

NOTE: To avoid long floats on the WS between color changes, twist the strand you are knitting with around the unused strand whenever there are more than 4 sts between color changes. Be careful not to pull the strand that floats.

RIGHT HAND MITTEN

With white CO 48 sts. Divide sts onto dpn and join, being careful not to twist cast-on row. Work 25 rnds k2, p2 ribbing in the following color sequence: 6 rnds white, 3 rnds black, 3 rnds white, 3 rnds black, 10 rnds white. Next, knit 1 rnd with white, increasing 9 sts evenly spaced around to 57 sts.

Now begin working charted pattern for right hand mitten. Use M1 to increase for the extra sts for the thumb gusset, knitting into the inc on the following rnd. On rnd 2, begin thumb gusset: k2, pm, M1, k1, M1, pm. On the next rnd, knit the new sts in pattern. Increase on rnds as indicated on chart until there are 13 sts for thumb gusset.

Annemor V709

On the rnd above the red line on the chart, remove markers, place the 13 sts underlined with red onto a holder for thumb and then CO 10 new sts following the pattern on the chart (CO with backward loop method) = 61 sts around.

Continue in charted pattern to top of mitten. The length of the mitten can be adjusted for either a woman's or man's size. Have the person who will wear the mitten try it on to make sure it fits.
Always work decreases with white. Decrease on each side of the contrast color lines up the sides of mitten. Work dec at right side of front (back) with ssk or sl 1-k1-psso; on the left side, k2tog. When 4 sts remain, cut yarn and pull tail through rem sts.

THUMB
Place the 13 sts from holder onto ndl and then, in pattern, pick up and knit 11 sts into CO row at top of thumbhole (use a crochet hook to pick up sts if necessary): 13 + 11 = 24 sts for thumb. Work following charted pattern for thumb, and, on the first rnd, k2tog at each side to avoid holes and for correct stitch count: 13 + 9 = 22 sts. Work until thumb is desired length; if necessary, work a few more rounds before shaping. Shape top of thumb as for top of mitten.

LEFT HAND MITTEN
Work as for right hand making sure that you follow the chart for Left Hand.

FINISHING
Weave in all tails neatly on WS. See page 25 for information on garment care.

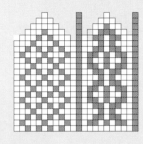

THUMB

RIGHT HAND

LEFT HAND

Eternal Love Mittens

The rose is the flower of love. Endless Roses is a decorative motif very much used in knitted art, both as a border and an allover pattern. There are no rules determining its height or width; the form of the mitten or the size of the hand determines the framework. Love and its representative pattern are similar in having no boundaries.

SIZE: WOMAN'S AND MAN'S
YARN: ASK HIFA 2 (SPORT, 100% WOOL, 344 YDS / 315 M, 100 G), 50 G WHITE 6057, 30 G GREY VIOLET 6079
NEEDLES: SET OF 4 OR 5 DPN U.S. SIZE 1.5 / 2.5 MM OR SIZE NEEDED TO OBTAIN GAUGE
GAUGE: 28 STS = 4 IN / 10 CM
STITCH COUNT: 56 STS AROUND HAND X APPROX 60 ROWS FOR LENGTH OF HAND

NOTE: To avoid long floats on the WS between color changes, twist the strand you are knitting with around the unused strand whenever there are more than 4 sts between color changes. Be careful not to pull the strand that floats.

RIGHT HAND MITTEN

With white CO 44 sts. Divide sts onto dpn and join, being careful not to twist cast-on row. Work in k2, p2 ribbing for approx 2½-2¾ in / 6-7 cm. Next, knit 1 rnd with white, increasing 6 sts evenly spaced around to 50 sts. Knit 1 more round and then add violet and work charted border pattern above cuff. After completing border, knit 2 rnds with white.

Now begin working charted pattern for right hand mitten. Use M1 to increase for the extra sts for the thumb gusset, knitting into the inc on the following rnd. On rnd 4, begin thumb gusset: k3, pm, M1, k3, M1, pm. On the next rnd, knit the new sts in pattern. Increase on rnds as indicated on chart until there are 11 sts for thumb gusset.

On the rnd above the red line on the chart, remove markers, place the 11 sts underlined with red onto a holder for thumb and then CO 11 new sts following the pattern on the chart (CO with backward loop method) = 56 sts around.

Continue in charted pattern to top of mitten. The length of the mitten can be adjusted for either a woman's or man's size. Have the person who will wear the mitten try it on to make sure it fits. Always work decreases with white. Decrease on each side of the contrast color lines up the sides of mitten. Work dec at right side of front (back) with ssk or sl 1-k1-psso; on the left side, k2tog. When 4 sts remain, cut yarn and pull tail through rem sts.

THUMB
Place the 11 sts from holder onto ndl and then, in pattern, pick up and knit 13 sts into CO row at top of thumbhole (use a crochet hook to pick up sts if necessary): 11 + 13 = 24 sts for thumb. Work following charted pattern for thumb, and, on the first rnd, k2tog at each side to avoid holes and for

correct stitch count: 11 + 11 = 22 sts. Work until thumb is desired length; if necessary, work a few more rounds before shaping. Shape top of thumb as for top of mitten.

LEFT HAND MITTEN
Work as for right hand making sure that you follow the chart for Left Hand.

FINISHING
Weave in all tails neatly on WS. See page 25 for information on garment care.

Annemor V786

**PATTERN BORDER
ABOVE CUFF**

RIGHT HAND

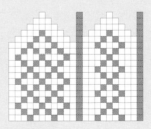

THUMB

LEFT HAND

Mittens with a Red Thread

A simple mitten landed unfinished in my rag pile. It had a red thread where the thumb should be. We'll never know if a relationship ended or maybe no one wanted the mitten. There is also a red thread in this mitten history – a red thread leading to new connections and renewed love. With your help, these mittens can be revived. No mitten should be knit in vain!

SIZE: WOMAN'S AND MAN'S

YARN: ASK HIFA 2 (SPORT, 100% WOOL, 344 YDS / 315 M, 100 G), 60 G TWEEDY BROWN 6102, 40 G WHITE 6057, SMALL AMOUNT OF RED 6014 IF DESIRED FOR CUFFS

NEEDLES: SET OF 4 OR 5 DPN U.S. SIZE 1.5 / 2.5 MM FOR MAN'S SIZE OR U.S. SIZE 0 / 2 MM FOR WOMAN'S SIZE; OR SIZE NEEDED TO OBTAIN GAUGE

GAUGE: 28 STS ON LARGER NDLS = 4 IN / 10 CM; 30 STS ON SMALLER NDLS = 4 IN / 10 CM

STITCH COUNT: 70 STS AROUND HAND X APPROX 70 ROWS FOR LENGTH OF HAND

NOTE: To avoid long floats on the WS between color changes, twist the strand you are knitting with around the unused strand whenever there are more than 4 sts between color changes. Be careful not to pull the strand that floats.

RIGHT HAND MITTEN

With brown CO 52 sts. Divide sts onto dpn and join, being careful not to twist cast-on row. Work 32 rnds in k2, p2 ribbing in color sequence (substitute red for white if desired): 8 rnds brown, 2 rnds white, 4 rnds brown, 2 rnds white, 16 rnds brown. Next, knit 1 rnd with brown, increasing 9 sts evenly spaced around to 61 sts. Now begin working charted pattern for right hand mitten. Use M1 to increase for the extra sts for the thumb gusset, knitting into the inc on the following rnd. On rnd 6, begin thumb gusset: k6, pm, M1, k1, M1, pm. On the next rnd, knit the new sts in pattern. Increase on rnds as indicated on chart until there are 13 sts for thumb gusset.

On the rnd above the red line on the chart, remove markers, place the 13 sts underlined with red onto

THUMB

RIGHT HAND

LEFT HAND

a holder for thumb and then CO 13 new sts following the pattern on the chart (CO with backward loop method) = 70 sts around.

Continue in charted pattern to top of mitten. The length of the mitten can be adjusted for either a woman's or man's size. Have the person who will wear the mitten try it on to make sure it fits. Always work decreases with brown. Decrease on each side of the contrast color lines up the sides of mitten. Work dec at right side of front (back) with ssk or sl 1-k1-psso; on the left side, k2tog. When 8 sts remain, cut yarn and pull tail through rem sts.

THUMB
Place the 13 sts from holder onto ndl and then, in pattern, pick up and knit 15 sts into CO row at top of thumbhole (use a crochet hook to pick up sts if necessary): 13 + 15 = 28 sts for thumb. Work following charted pattern for thumb, and, on the first rnd, k2tog at each side to avoid holes and for correct stitch count: 13 + 13 = 26 sts. Work until thumb is desired length; if necessary, work a few more rounds before shaping. Shape top of thumb as follows: decrease at right side of front (back) with ssk or sl 1-k1-psso; on the left side, k2tog.

When 4 sts rem, cut yarn and pull tail through rem sts.

LEFT HAND MITTEN
Work as for right hand making sure that you follow the chart for Left Hand.

FINISHING
Weave in all tails neatly on WS. See page 25 for information on garment care.

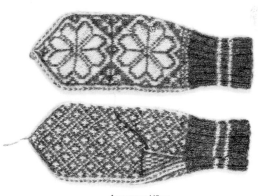

Annemor V897

87

Spider Mittens

The spider is a fortuitous animal in folk beliefs. He spins a cosmic web and weaves the fate of people caught in the world's pattern. The spider is at the center of the mitten with a cross on its back and the spokes of its web stream out to all the edges like the sun's rays. Within the web evergreen branches intertwine with love's endless roses.

SIZE: ADULT
YARN: ASK HIFA 2 (SPORT, 100% WOOL, 344 YDS / 315 M, 100 G), 60 G MEDIUM BLUE 6035 AND 30 G WHITE 6057
NEEDLES: SET OF 4 OR 5 DPN U.S. SIZE 1.5 / 2.5 MM
GAUGE: 28 STS = 4 IN / 10 CM
STITCH COUNT: 68 STS AROUND HAND X APPROX 70 ROWS FOR LENGTH OF HAND

NOTE: To avoid long floats on the WS between color changes, twist the strand you are knitting with around the unused strand whenever there are more than 4 sts between color changes. Be careful not to pull in the floating strand on WS.

RIGHT HAND MITTEN

With blue, CO 60 sts; divide onto dpn and join, being careful not to twist cast-on row. Work 2 rnds in k1, p1 ribbing and then knit 1 rnd. Add white and work charted cuff pattern.

After completing cuff chart, knit one rnd with blue, increasing 2 sts evenly spaced around = 62 sts. Knit 2 rnds with blue.

Begin charted pattern for right hand mitten. On rnd 5, begin thumb gusset: K3, pm, M1, k5, M1, pm. On the next rnd, knit the new sts in pattern. Increase on rnds as indicated on chart until there are 13 sts for thumb gusset.

On the rnd above the red line on the chart, remove markers and place the 13 sts underlined with red onto a holder for thumb and then CO 13 new sts following the pattern on the chart (CO with backward loop method) = 68 sts around.

Continue in charted pattern up to shaping for top of mitten. Always work decreases with blue on each side of the white lines up sides of mitten. Work dec at right side (immediately after the white line) of front (back) with ssk or sl 1-k1-psso; on the left side (after the white line), k2tog. When 4 sts remain, cut yarn and pull tail through rem sts.

THUMB
Place the 13 sts from holder onto ndl and then, in pattern, pick up and knit 15 sts into CO row at top of thumbhole (use a crochet hook to pick up sts if necessary). Work following the thumb chart; on the first rnd, k2tog at each side to avoid holes and for correct stitch count = 13 + 13 = 26 sts for thumb. Work to thumb shaping. If the thumb

Annemor V986

is too short at this point (it should reach middle of thumbnail), work more rounds as needed for desired thumb length. Shape top of thumb as for top of mitten.

LEFT HAND MITTEN
Work as for right hand making sure that you follow the chart for Left Hand.

FINISHING
Weave in all tails neatly on WS. See page 25 for information on garment care.

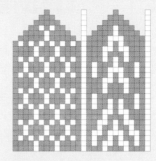

THUMB

RIGHT

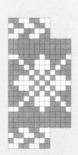

CUFF BORDER

LEFT HAND

Mittens with a Twist

Many of the mittens I've found can be traced back to a specific pattern or they were knit following to the strict rules of a particular knitting tradition. The knitter of this pair seems to have been in a "mitten-or-glove" dilemma. The hand begins with a typical reindeer for gloves and finishes with a mitten motif. For that reason it seems like the knitter followed the advice of my grandmother and made the reindeer design in her own style.

SIZE: ADULT

YARN: ASK HIFA 2 (SPORT, 100% WOOL, 344 YDS / 315 M, 100 G), 40 G HUNTER'S GREEN 6089, 25 G HEATHERY LIGHT GRAY 6054

NEEDLES: SET OF 4 OR 5 DPN U.S. SIZE 1.5 / 2.5 MM OR SIZE NEEDED TO OBTAIN GAUGE

GAUGE: 28 STS = 4 IN / 10 CM

STITCH COUNT: 56 STS AROUND HAND X APPROX 60 ROWS FOR LENGTH OF HAND

NOTE: To avoid long floats on the WS between color changes, twist the strand you are knitting with around the unused strand whenever there are more than 4 sts between color changes. Be careful not to pull in the floating strand on WS.

RIGHT HAND MITTEN

With light gray, CO 45 sts; divide onto dpn and join, being careful not to twist cast-on row. Work 31 rnds in k4 tbl, p1 ribbing in the following color sequence: 7 rnds light gray, 2 rnds green, 4 rnds light gray, (1 rnd green, 1 rnd light gray) 3 times, 1 rnd green, 4 rnds light gray, 2 rnds green, 5 rnds light gray. (Note that the original mitten was worked with k4, p1 ribbing, not twisted knit stitches). Knit 1 rnd with light gray, and, at the same time, increase 5 sts evenly spaced around = 50 sts.

Begin charted pattern for right hand mitten. On rnd 7, begin thumb gusset: K4, pm, M1, k3, M1,

Annemor V711.13

pm. On the next rnd, knit the new sts in pattern. Increase on rnds as indicated on chart until there are 14 sts for thumb gusset.

On the rnd above the red line on the chart, remove markers and place the 14 sts underlined with red onto a holder for thumb and then CO 11 new sts following the pattern on the chart (CO with backward loop method)= 56 sts around.

Continue in charted pattern up to shaping for top of mitten. Always work decreases with white on each side of the contrast color lines up sides of mitten. Work dec at right side of front (back) with ssk or sl 1-k1-psso; on the left side, k2tog. When 4 sts remain, cut yarn and pull tail through rem sts.

THUMB

Place the 14 sts from holder onto ndl and then, in pattern, pick up and knit 12 sts into CO row at top of thumbhole (use a crochet hook to pick up sts if necessary): 14 + 12 = 26 sts for thumb. Work following the thumb chart; on the first rnd, k2tog at each side to avoid holes and for correct stitch count = 14 + 10 = 24 sts. Work to thumb shaping. If the thumb is too short at this point (it should reach middle of thumbnail), work more rounds as needed for desired thumb length. Shape top of thumb as for top of mitten.

LEFT HAND MITTEN

Work as for right hand making sure that you follow the chart for Left Hand.

FINISHING

Weave in all tails neatly on WS. See page 25 for information on garment care.

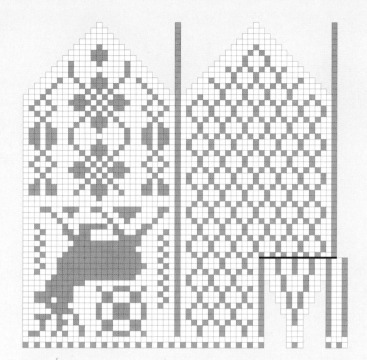

THUMB

RIGHT HAND

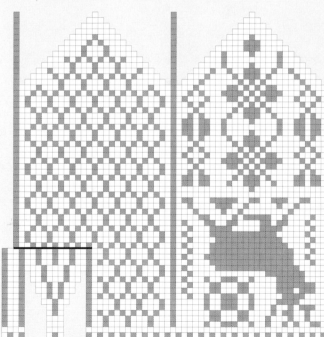

LEFT HAND

The Ash Lad

At first I called the motif on this mitten the "bird man" but then I changed it to the "water bearer." Later, it struck me that he had two matching billy goat horns like "Askeladden," the Ash Lad in an old Norwegian folktale and, so, I decided to call him the "Ash Lad" in honor of the Ask or Ash yarn from Hillesvåg Woolens that my gloves are knit with.

SIZE: CHILD'S
YARN: ASK HIFA 2 (SPORT, 100% WOOL, 344 YDS / 315 M, 100 G), 35 G BLUE-GREEN 6086, 16 G LIGHT GRAY 6106
NEEDLES: SET OF 4 OR 5 DPN U.S. SIZE 1.5 / 2.5 MM OR SIZE NEEDED TO OBTAIN GAUGE
GAUGE: 28 STS = 4 IN / 10 CM
STITCH COUNT: 52 STS AROUND HAND

NOTE: To avoid long floats on the WS between color changes, twist the strand you are knitting with around the unused strand whenever there are more than 4 sts between color changes. Be careful not to pull the strand that floats.

RIGHT HAND GLOVE

With blue-green, CO 40 sts; divide onto dpn and join, being careful not to twist cast-on row. Work 22 rnds k2, p2 ribbing (or, if you prefer the original mittens, k3, p1) in the following color sequence: 6 rnds blue-green, 2 rnds light gray, 2 rnds blue-green, 2 rnds light gray, 2 rnds blue-green, 2 rnds light gray, 6 rnds blue-green. Finish cuff by knit-ting 1 rnd with blue-green and, at the same time, increase 8 sts evenly spaced around = 48 sts. Knit 8 rnds with blue-green.

Now begin working charted pattern for right hand glove. Use M1 to increase for the extra sts for the thumb gusset, knitting into the inc on the following rnd. On rnd 4, begin thumb gusset: K4, pm, M1, k1, M1, pm. On the next rnd, knit the new sts in pattern. Increase on rnds as indicated on chart until there are 10 sts for thumb gusset.

On the rnd above the red line on the chart, remove markers and place the 10 sts underlined with red onto a holder for thumb and then CO 8 new sts following the pattern on the chart (CO with backward loop method) = 52 sts around.

Continue in charted pattern to the base of the fingers. Place hand sts on a holder while you knit the thumb. Thumb and fingers are worked with blue-green.

97

RIGHT HAND

LEFT HAND

Annemor V711.19

THUMB

Place the 10 sts from holder onto ndl and then, with blue-green, pick up and knit 10 sts into CO row at top of thumbhole (use a crochet hook to pick up sts if necessary): 10 + 10 = 20 sts for thumb. Work thumb in stockinette, and, on the first rnd, k2tog at each side to avoid holes and for correct stitch count: 10 + 8 = 18 sts. Try on the glove to make sure the thumb is long enough (it should reach middle of thumbnail); work more rounds as needed for desired thumb length. On the glove shown the thumb is 1½ in / 4 cm long before shaping. Shape top of thumb as follows: decrease at right side of front (back) with ssk or sl 1-k1-psso; on the left side, k2tog. When 2-4 sts rem, cut yarn and pull tail through rem sts.

INDEX FINGER

Place 7 sts from the back of the hand + 1 side st + 6 sts from palm onto ndls and CO 2 sts with backwards loop method at base of middle finger = 16 sts total. Knit around in stockinette until finger is about 1½ in / 4 cm long or desired length and then shape top as for thumb.

MIDDLE FINGER

Place 7 sts from the back of the hand onto dpn, pick up and knit 2 sts from cast-on at base of index finger, place 7 sts from palm onto ndl, and CO 2 sts with backwards loop method at base of ring finger = 18 sts total. Knit around in stockinette until finger is about 2½ in / 6 cm long or desired length and then shape top as for thumb.

RING FINGER

Place 6 sts from the back of the hand onto dpn, pick up and knit 2 sts from cast-on at base of middle finger, place 6 sts from palm onto ndl, and CO 2 sts with backwards loop method at base of little finger = 16 sts total. Knit around in stockinette until finger is about 1½ in / 4 cm long or until finger is desired length and then shape top as for thumb.

LITTLE FINGER

Place rem sts = 6 from back of hand + 1 side st + 7 sts from palm and then pick up and knit 2 sts along cast-on at base of ring finger = total of 16 sts. Knit around in stockinette until finger is about 1¼ in / 3.5 cm long or desired length and the shape top as for thumb.

LEFT HAND GLOVE

Work as for right hand making sure that you follow the chart for Left Hand and place thumb and fingers correctly.

FINISHING

Weave in all tails neatly on WS. See page 25 for information on garment care.

Olive Mittens

The olive branch or twig conveys messages about benedictions and peace. Stories about Noah's Ark, tell us that a dove came back to the ark with an olive branch in its beak to show that the water had gone down after the huge flood. The olive tree can grow for centuries and thus also symbolizes longevity.

SIZE: ADULT
YARN: ASK HIFA 2 (SPORT, 100% WOOL, 344 YDS / 315 M, 100 G), 60 G WHITE 6057 AND 45 G BROWN 6099
NEEDLES: SET OF 4 OR 5 DPN U.S. SIZE 1.5 / 2.5 MM OR SIZE NEEDED TO OBTAIN GAUGE
GAUGE: 28 STS = 4 IN / 10 CM
STITCH COUNT: 72 STS AROUND HAND X APPROX 78 ROWS FOR LENGTH OF HAND — OR, IF USING THE ALTERNATE SHAPING FOR TOP OF HAND, APPROX 70 ROWS (SEE CHARTED OPTIONS ON P. 103).

NOTE: To avoid long floats on the WS between color changes, twist the strand you are knitting with around the unused strand whenever there are more than 4 sts between color changes. Be careful not to pull the strand that floats.

RIGHT HAND MITTEN
With white, CO 56 sts; divide onto dpn and join, being careful not to twist cast-on row. Work 33 rnds in k2, p2 ribbing in the following color sequence: 6 rnds white, (1 rnd brown, 1 rnd white, 3 rnds brown, 1 rnd white, 1 rnd brown, 3 rnds white) 2 times, 1 rnd brown, 1 rnd white, 3 rnds brown, 1 rnd white, 1 rnd brown. Finish cuff by knitting 1 rnd with white and, at the same time, increase 8 sts evenly spaced around = 64 sts. Knit 1 more rnd with white.

Now begin working charted pattern for right hand mitten. On rnd 5 of hand, begin thumb gusset: K6, pm, M1, k1, M1, pm. Use M1 to increase for the extra sts for the thumb gusset, knitting into the inc on the following rnd. Increase on rnds as indicated on chart until there are 17 sts for thumb gusset. On the rnd above the red line on the chart, remove markers, place the 17 sts underlined with red onto a holder for thumb and then CO 15 new sts following the pattern on the chart (CO with backward loop method) = 72 sts around.

Annemor V1068

Continue in charted pattern to top of mitten. Try on mitten to make sure it will be long enough – it should reach the top of the little finger. If necessary work a few more rounds before shaping. Always work decreases with white. Decrease on each side of the contrast color lines up the sides of mitten. Work dec at right side (just after dividing line at side) of front (back) with ssk or sl 1-k1-psso; on the left side (before dividing line), k2tog. When 8 sts remain, cut yarn and pull tail through rem sts.

THUMB

Place the 17 sts from holder onto ndl and then, in pattern, pick up and knit 17 sts into CO row at top of thumbhole (use a crochet hook to pick up sts if necessary): 17 + 17 = 34 sts for thumb. Work following the thumb chart; on the first rnd, k2tog at each side to avoid holes and for correct stitch count: 17 + 15 = 32 sts. Try on mitten to make sure thumb is long enough – it should reach to middle of thumbnail. If necessary, work a few more rounds before shaping top. Shape top of thumb as for top of mitten. When 8 sts remain, cut yarn and pull through rem sts.

NOTE: The thumb for the woman's size may need to be shortened. You can also decrease the stitch count for a narrower thumb by working 1 contrast color stitch (instead of 3) at each side of the thumb.

LEFT HAND MITTEN

Work as for right hand making sure that you follow the chart for Left Hand.

FINISHING

Weave in all tails neatly on WS. See page 25 for information on garment care.

THUMB

RIGHT HAND

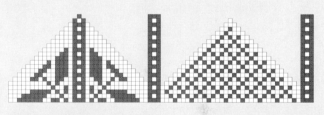

ALTERNATIVE TOP SHAPING

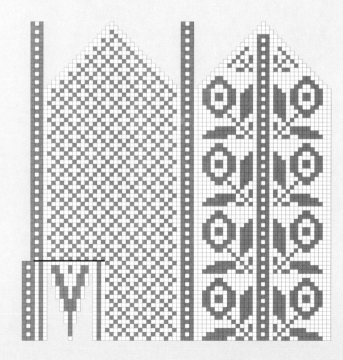

LEFT HAND

Flørnes Dog

Here's a mitten from the Selbu tradition that is richly decorated with several motifs. If you copy the mitten on a copy machine, you can cut out each of the motifs separately and then rearrange and repeat them for single motifs, borders and allover patterns. You'll find a treasure chest full of patterns in one mitten, a pattern bank that can be used for new knitwear. For example, you can use the motifs as the starting point for a glove and then decide if you want plain or patterned fingers.

Annemor V711.4

SIZE: MAN'S
YARN: ASK HIFA 2 (SPORT, 100% WOOL, 344 YDS / 315 M, 100 G), 60 G WHITE 6057 AND 40 G DARK GRAY-BLUE 6104
NEEDLES: SET OF 4 OR 5 DPN U.S. SIZE 1.5 / 2.5 MM OR SIZE NEEDED TO OBTAIN GAUGE
GAUGE: 28 STS = 4 IN / 10 CM
STITCH COUNT: 68 STS AROUND HAND X APPROX 70 ROWS FOR LENGTH OF HAND

NOTE: To avoid long floats on the WS between color changes, twist the strand you are knitting with around the unused strand whenever there are more than 4 sts between color changes. Be careful not to pull the strand that floats.

THUMB

RIGHT HAND

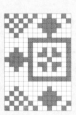

CUFF

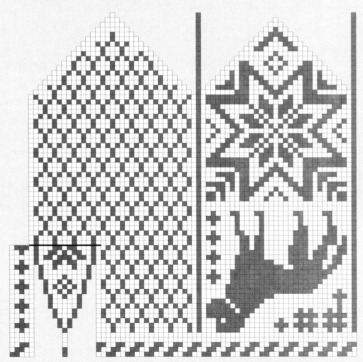

LEFT HAND

RIGHT HAND MITTEN

With white, CO 56 sts; divide onto dpn and join, being careful not to twist cast-on row. Work 3 rnds k1, p1 ribbing and then knit 1 rnd with white. Add grey-blue and work cuff pattern – the 14-stitch repeat is worked 4 times around. After completing cuff chart rows, knit 1 rnd with white, and, at the same time, increase 4 sts evenly spaced around = 60 sts. Knit 1 rnd with white.

Now begin working charted pattern for right hand mitten. On rnd 7 of hand, begin thumb gusset: K5, pm, M1, k1, M1, pm. Use M1 to increase for the extra sts for the thumb gusset, knitting into the inc on the following rnd. Increase on rnds as indicated on chart until there are 16 sts for thumb gusset. On the rnd above the red line on the chart, remove markers, place the 15 sts underlined with red onto a holder for thumb and then CO 11 new sts following the pattern on the chart (CO with backward loop method) = 68 sts around.

Continue in charted pattern to top of mitten. Try on mitten to make sure it will be long enough – it should reach the top of the little finger. If necessary work a few more rounds before shaping. Al-ways work decreases with white. Decrease on each side of the contrast color lines up the sides of mitten. Work dec at right side (just after dividing line at side) of front (back) with ssk or sl 1-k1-psso; on the left side (before dividing line), k2tog. When 4 sts remain, cut yarn and pull tail through rem sts.

THUMB

Place the 15 sts from holder onto ndl and then, in pattern, pick up and knit 13 sts into CO row at top of thumbhole (use a crochet hook to pick up sts if necessary): 15 + 13 = 28 sts for thumb. Work following the thumb chart. Try on mitten to make sure thumb is long enough – it should reach to middle of thumbnail. If necessary, work a few more rounds before shaping top. Shape top of thumb as for top of mitten. When 4 sts remain, cut yarn and pull tail through rem sts.

LEFT HAND MITTEN

Work as for right hand making sure that you follow the chart for Left Hand.

FINISHING

Weave in all tails neatly on WS. See page 25 for information on garment care.

107

Daddy Longlegs

Large, living spiders are often frightening, but in some folk beliefs, spiders denote good fortune. Just as beloved children have many names, a spider in Norway might be called a kongro, klung, vevkjerring (daddy longlegs) or spinnar (spinner), depending on the dialect. These gloves have the biggest spider I've seen in knitting. A real spider can vary in size from as little as 1/16 to 9¾ in long (a few millimeters to more than 25 cm). The biggest ones might weigh up to 5.3 ounces / 150 g and live for 40 years. So, a pair of gloves with this spider motif will bring wishes for good luck to several generations.

SIZE: WOMAN'S AND MAN'S
YARN: ASK HIFA 2 (SPORT, 100% WOOL, 344 YDS / 315 M, 100 G), 60 G DARK BROWN 6010, 30 G 6057
NEEDLES: SET OF 4 OR 5 DPN U.S. SIZE 1.5 / 2.5 MM OR U.S. SIZE 0 / 2 MM FOR WOMAN'S GLOVES) OR SIZE NEEDED TO OBTAIN GAUGE.
GAUGE: 28 STS ON LARGER NEEDLES = 4 IN / 10 CM; 30 STS ON SMALLER NEEDLES = 4 IN / 10 CM
STITCH COUNT: 68 STS AROUND HAND X APPROX 70 ROWS FOR LENGTH OF HAND

NOTE: To avoid long floats on the WS between color changes, twist the strand you are knitting with around the unused strand whenever there are more than 4 sts between color changes. Be careful not to pull the strand that floats.

RIGHT HAND GLOVE

With dark brown, CO 52 sts; divide onto dpn and join, being careful not to twist cast-on row. Work 30 rnds k1, p1 ribbing in the following color sequence: 12 rnds brown, 2 rnds white, 3 rnds brown, 1 rnd white, 12 rnds brown, 1 rnd white. Finish cuff by knitting 1 rnd with brown and, at the same time, increase 8 sts evenly spaced around = 60 sts. Knit 2 rnds with brown.

Now begin working charted pattern for right hand glove. Use M1 to increase for the extra sts for the thumb gusset, knitting into the inc on the following rnd. On rnd 2, begin thumb gusset: K4, pm, M1, k1, M1, pm. On the next rnd, knit the new sts in pattern. Increase on rnds as indicated on chart until there are 14 sts for thumb gusset.

Annemor V1060.4

On the rnd above the red line on the chart, remove markers and place the 14 sts underlined with red onto a holder for thumb and then CO 12 new sts following the pattern on the chart (CO with backward loop method) = 68 sts around.

Continue in charted pattern to the base of the fingers. Place hand sts on a holder while you knit the thumb.

THUMB
Place the 14 sts from holder onto ndl and then, in pattern, pick up and knit 14 sts into CO row at top of thumbhole (use a crochet hook to pick up sts if necessary): 14 + 14 = 28 sts for thumb. Work thumb in charted pattern, and, on the first rnd, k2tog at each side to avoid holes and for correct stitch count: 14 + 12 = 26 sts. Try on the glove to make sure the thumb is long enough (it should reach middle of thumbnail); work more rounds as needed for desired thumb length. Shape top of thumb as follows: decrease at right side of front (back) with ssk or sl 1-k1-psso; on the left side, k2tog. When 4 sts rem, cut yarn and pull tail through rem sts.

INDEX FINGER
Place 10 sts from the back of the hand + 1 side st + 9 sts from palm onto ndls and CO 5 sts with backwards loop method at base of middle finger =

25 sts total. Knit following chart for index finger; add rows if necessary for desired length and then shape top as for thumb.

MIDDLE FINGER
Place 8 sts from the back of the hand onto dpn, pick up and knit 5 sts from cast-on at base of index finger, place 8 sts from palm onto ndl, and CO 4 sts with backwards loop method at base of ring finger = 25 sts total. Knit following chart for middle finger; add rows if necessary for desired length and then shape top as for thumb.

RING FINGER
Place 8 sts from the back of the hand onto dpn, pick up and knit 4 sts from cast-on at base of middle finger, place 8 sts from palm onto ndl, and CO 5 sts with backwards loop method at base of little finger = 25 sts total. Knit following chart for ring finger; add rows if necessary for desired length and then shape top as for thumb.

LITTLE FINGER
Place rem sts = 8 from back of hand + 1 side st + 7 sts from palm and then pick up and knit 6 sts along cast-on at base of ring finger = total of 22 sts. Knit around in stockinette until finger is about 2 in / 5 cm long or desired length and then shape top as for thumb.

LEFT HAND GLOVE
Work as for right hand making sure that you follow the chart for Left Hand and place thumb and fingers correctly.

FINISHING
Weave in all tails neatly on WS. See page 25 for information on garment care.

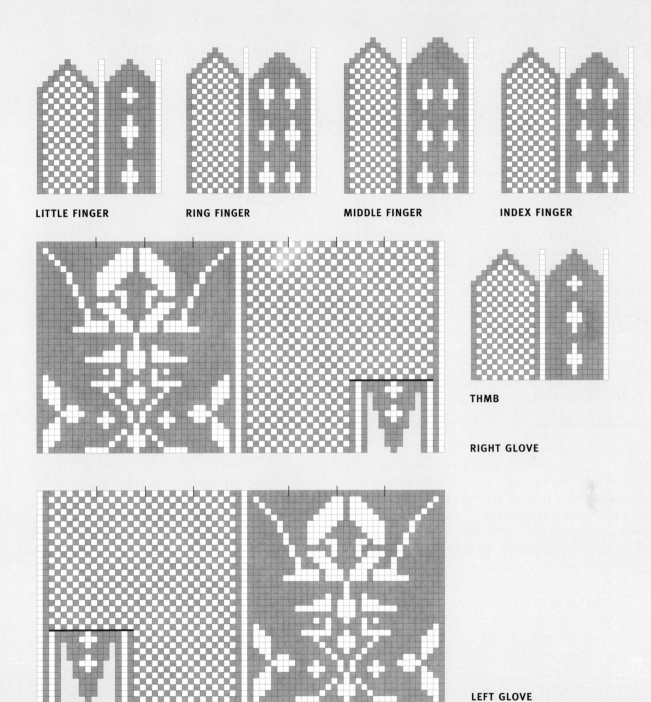

LITTLE FINGER

RING FINGER

MIDDLE FINGER

INDEX FINGER

THMB

RIGHT GLOVE

LEFT GLOVE

Starfish

Eight-pointed stars are a common knitting motif with many variations. The star pattern on these mittens is often found on Norwegian Fana sweaters. Since it's called a "starfish" in English, it can be included in my animal-themed book of mittens and gloves.

SIZE: CHILD'S
YARN: ASK HIFA 2 (SPORT, 100% WOOL, 344 YDS / 315 M, 100 G), 30 G DEEP ROSE 6068, 20 G WHITE 6057
NEEDLES: SET OF 4 OR 5 DPN U.S. SIZE 1.5 / 2.5 MM OR SIZE NEEDED TO OBTAIN GAUGE
GAUGE: 28 STS = 4 IN / 10 CM
STITCH COUNT: 48 STS AROUND HAND X APPROX 43 ROWS FOR LENGTH OF HAND

NOTE: To avoid long floats on the WS between color changes, twist the strand you are knitting with around the unused strand whenever there are more than 4 sts between color changes. Be careful not to pull the strand that floats.

RIGHT HAND MITTEN
With rose, CO 40 sts; divide onto dpn and join, being careful not to twist cast-on row. Work in k2, p2 ribbing for about 2 in / 5 cm. After completing cuff, knit 1 rnd with rose, and, at the same time, increase 5 sts evenly spaced around = 45 sts.

Now begin working charted pattern for right hand mitten. On rnd 3 of hand, begin thumb gusset: K5, pm, M1, pm. Use M1 to increase for the extra sts for the thumb gusset, knitting into the inc on the following rnd. Increase on rnds as indicated on chart until there are 11 sts for thumb gusset.

On the rnd above the red line on the chart, remove markers, place the 11 sts underlined with red onto a holder for thumb and then CO 9 new sts following the pattern on the chart (CO with backward loop method) = 48 sts around.

Continue in charted pattern to top of mitten. Try on mitten to make sure it will be long enough – it should reach the top of the little finger. If necessary work a few more rounds before shaping. Always work decreases with rose and read note under chart for specifs on which stitches to join for decreases. Decrease on each side of the contrast color lines up the sides of mitten. Work dec at right side (just after dividing line at side) of front (back)

THUMB

RIGHT HAND

When shaping top of mitten hands and thumbs, make sure that the rose side stitch is knitted together with a side stitch from the palm and the white side stitch is knitted together with a side stitch from the back of hand.

LEFT HAND

with ssk or sl 1-k1-psso; on the left side (before dividing line), k2tog. When 6 sts remain, cut yarn and pull tail through rem sts.

THUMB
Place the 11 sts from holder onto ndl and then, in pattern, pick up and knit 11 sts into CO row at top of thumbhole (use a crochet hook to pick up sts if necessary): 11 + 11 = 22 sts for thumb. Work following the thumb chart. Try on mitten to make sure thumb is long enough – it should reach to middle of thumbnail. If necessary, work a few more rounds before shaping top. Shape top of thumb as for top of mitten. When 6 sts remain, cut yarn and pull tail through rem sts.

LEFT HAND MITTEN
Work as for right hand making sure that you follow the chart for Left Hand.

FINISHING
Weave in all tails neatly on WS. See page 25 for information on garment care.

Annemor V878.11

115

Odin's Ravens Hugin and Mugin

Odin's ravens, Hugin and Mugin represent tidings and memory. I loaned this child's mitten to Terri Shea for her book, *Selbuvotter: Biography of a Knitting Tradition*. This symbolizes, for me, the emigrants who took new chances in a new country, and immigrants who looked back at their memories and traditions. I've reworked the mitten for adult and large child's sizes so that everyone can be made happy by wearing these mittens – the raven design represents both looking forward and looking back.

SIZE: CHILD'S
YARN: ASK HIFA 2 (SPORT, 100% WOOL, 344 YDS / 315 M, 100 G), 50 G BLACK 6053, 50 G WHITE 6057
NEEDLES: SET OF 4 OR 5 DPN U.S. SIZE 1.5 / 2.5 MM OR SIZE NEEDED TO OBTAIN GAUGE
GAUGE: 28 STS = 4 IN / 10 CM
STITCH COUNT: 50 STS AROUND HAND X APPROX 48 ROWS FOR LENGTH OF HAND

NOTE: To avoid long floats on the WS between color changes, twist the strand you are knitting with around the unused strand whenever there are more than 4 sts between color changes. Be careful not to pull the strand that floats.

RIGHT HAND MITTEN

With white, CO 40 sts; divide onto dpn and join, being careful not to twist cast-on row. Purl 1 rnd and then work 2 rnds of k1, p1 ribbing. Next, work charted cuff pattern, and, on the last round, increase 6 sts evenly spaced around = 46 sts.
Before you begin the hand pattern, knit 1 rnd with white, and, at the same time, increase 1 st to 47 sts total; knit 1 more rnd with white.

Now begin working charted pattern for right hand mitten. On rnd 4 of hand, begin thumb gusset: K5, pm, M1, k1, M1, pm. Use M1 to increase for the extra sts for the thumb gusset, knitting into the inc on the following rnd. Increase on rnds as indicated on chart until there are 13 sts for thumb gusset.

Annemor V710

On the rnd above the red line on the chart, remove markers, place the 13 sts underlined with red onto a holder for thumb and then CO 8 new sts following the pattern on the chart (CO with backward loop method) = 50 sts around.

Continue in charted pattern to top of mitten. Try on mitten to make sure it will be long enough – it should reach the top of the little finger. If necessary work a few more rounds before shaping. Always work decreases with white. Decrease on each side of the contrast color lines up the sides of mitten. Work dec at right side (just after dividing line at side) of front (back) with ssk or sl 1-k1-psso; on the left side (before dividing line), k2tog. When 4 sts remain, cut yarn and pull tail through rem sts.

THUMB

Place the 13 sts from holder onto ndl and then, in pattern, pick up and knit 9 sts into CO row at top of thumbhole (use a crochet hook to pick up sts if necessary): 13 + 9 = 22 sts for thumb. Work following the thumb chart, and on the first rnd, k2tog at each side to avoid holes and for correct stitch count: 13 + 7 = 20 sts. Try on mitten to make sure thumb is long enough – it should reach to middle of thumbnail. If necessary, work a few more rounds before shaping top. Shape top of thumb as for top of mitten. When 4 sts remain, cut yarn and pull tail through rem sts.

LEFT HAND MITTEN

Work as for right hand making sure that you follow the chart for Left Hand.

FINISHING

Weave in all tails neatly on WS. See page 25 for information on garment care.

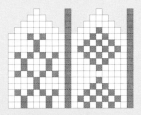

THUMB

RIGHT HAND

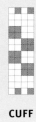

CUFF

LEFT HAND

Odin's Ravens Hugin and Mugin

SIZE: ADULT
YARN: EMBLA HIFA 3 (DK, 100% WOOL, 229 YDS, / 210 M, 100 G), 50 G BLACK 6053, 50 G WHITE 6057
NEEDLES: SET OF 4 OR 5 DPN U.S. SIZE 2.5 / 3 MM OR SIZE NEEDED TO OBTAIN GAUGE
GAUGE: 24 STS = 4 IN / 10 CM
STITCH COUNT: 64 STS AROUND HAND X APPROX 58 ROWS FOR LENGTH OF HAND

NOTE: To avoid long floats on the WS between color changes, twist the strand you are knitting with around the unused strand whenever there are more than 4 sts between color changes. Be careful not to pull the strand that floats.

RIGHT HAND MITTEN
With white, CO 52 sts; divide onto dpn and join, being careful not to twist cast-on row. Work 2 rnds of k1, p1 ribbing and then knit 1 rnd with white. Next, add black and work charted cuff pattern. After completing cuff pattern, work 1 rnd with white, and, at the same time, increase 7 sts evenly spaced around = 59 sts. Knit 1 more rnd with white.

Now begin working charted pattern for right hand mitten. On rnd 4 of hand, begin thumb gusset: K6, pm, M1, k1, M1, pm. Use M1 to increase for the extra sts for the thumb gusset, knitting into the inc on the following rnd. Increase on rnds as indicated on chart until there are 16 sts for thumb gusset. On the rnd above the red line on the chart, remove markers, place the 16 sts underlined with red onto a holder for thumb and then CO 11 new sts following the pattern on the chart (CO with backward loop method) = 64 sts around.

Continue in charted pattern to top of mitten. Try on mitten to make sure it will be long enough – it should reach the top of the little finger. If necessary work a few more rounds before shaping. Always work decreases with white. Decrease on each side of the contrast color lines up the sides of mitten. Work dec at right side (just after dividing line at side) of front (back) with ssk or sl 1-k1-psso; on the left side (before dividing line), k2tog. When 6 sts remain, cut yarn and pull tail through rem sts.

THUMB

Place the 16 sts from holder onto ndl and then, in pattern, pick up and knit 12 sts into CO row at top of thumbhole (use a crochet hook to pick up sts if necessary): 16 + 12 = 28 sts for thumb. Work following the thumb chart, and on the first rnd, k2tog at each side to avoid holes and for correct stitch count: 15 + 11 = 26 sts. Try on mitten to make sure thumb is long enough – it should reach to middle of thumbnail. If necessary, work a few more rounds before shaping top. Shape top of thumb as for top of mitten. When 4 sts remain, cut yarn and pull tail through rem sts.

LEFT HAND MITTEN

Work as for right hand making sure that you follow the chart for Left Hand.

FINISHING

Weave in all tails neatly on WS. See page 25 for information on garment care.

When the pattern on the back of the thumb is not symmetrical, it should be worked mirror-image (that is, work it as on the chart for one thumb but in reverse on the other).

THUMB

RIGHT HAND

CUFF

LEFT HAND

Frolicking Rabbits

These were originally small sized machine-knit mittens that I reworked for hand knitting. I borrowed the motifs and borders from the original and changed some colors to create a new hand knit variation. Rabbits represent innocence and the defenseless. In the art of knitting it is well known as a delightful motif for children but in medieval art the rabbit was a symbol of material and carnal desires.

SIZE: SMALL CHILD

YARN: ASK HIFA 2 (SPORT, 100% WOOL, 344 YDS / 315 M, 100 G), 30 G BROWN 6099, 20 G GREEN 6086, 10 G EACH WHITE 6057, YELLOW 6002, RED 6014 (OR USE YOUR COLOR CHOICE OF LEFTOVER YARNS FOR THE CONTRAST COLORS)

NEEDLES: SET OF 4 OR 5 DPN U.S. SIZE 1.5 / 2.5 MM OR SIZE NEEDED TO OBTAIN GAUGE

GAUGE: 28 STS = 4 IN / 10 CM

STITCH COUNT: 43 STS AROUND HAND X APPROX 47 ROWS FOR LENGTH OF HAND

NOTE: To avoid long floats on the WS between color changes, twist the strand you are knitting with around the unused strand whenever there are more than 4 sts between color changes. Be careful not to pull the strand that floats.

RIGHT HAND MITTEN

With green, CO 40 sts; divide onto dpn and join, being careful not to twist cast-on row. Work in k1, p1 ribbing for about 1½ in / 4 cm. Before beginning charted pattern for hand, knit 2 rnds with black (increasing 3 sts evenly spaced around to 43 sts on the first rnd) and then knit 2 rnds with brown.

Now begin working charted pattern for right hand mitten. On the rnd above the black line on the chart, place the 8 sts underlined with black onto a holder for thumb and then CO 8 new sts over the gap following the pattern on the chart (CO with backward loop method) = 43 sts around.

Continue in charted pattern to top of mitten. Try on mitten to make sure it will be long enough – it

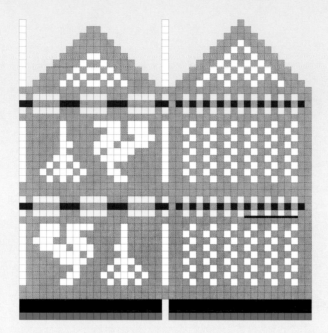

RIGHT HAND

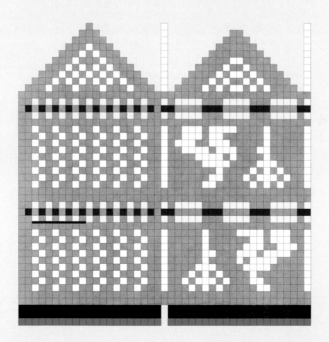

LEFT HAND

should reach the top of the little finger. If necessary work a few more rounds before shaping. Always work decreases with brown. Decrease on each side of the contrast color lines up the sides of mitten. Work dec at right side (just after dividing line at side) of front (back) with ssk or sl 1-k1-psso; on the left side (before dividing line), k2tog. When 4 sts remain, cut yarn and pull tail through rem sts.

THUMB
Place the 8 sts from holder onto ndl and knit them with black; next, pick up and knit 10 sts into CO row at top of thumbhole (use a crochet hook to pick up sts if necessary): 8 + 10 = 18 sts for thumb. Knit a second rnd with black, and k2tog at each side to avoid holes and for correct stitch count: 8 + 8 = 16 sts. Cut black and knit the rest of the thumb with green. Try on mitten to make sure thumb is long enough – it should reach to middle of thumbnail. If necessary, work a few more rounds before shaping top. Shape top of thumb as for top of mitten, decreasing at each side. When 2-4 sts remain, cut yarn and pull tail through rem sts.

LEFT HAND MITTEN
Work as for right hand making sure that you follow the chart for Left Hand.

FINISHING
Weave in all tails neatly on WS. See page 25 for information on garment care.

Annemor V555.4

127

Squirrel and Hare

This purchased pair of small gloves inspired me to rework it for hand knitting. I chose to make it for both small and large children. The squirrel symbolizes different things in different cultures. In Norse mythology he is the "ratatosken" who ran up and down the world's tree, Yggdrasil, with gossip between the rats and eagles in the top branches. On these mittens, the squirrels have no deeper meaning than a playful child's motif.

SIZE: SMALL CHILD

YARN: ASK HIFA 2 (SPORT, 100% WOOL, 344 YDS / 315 M, 100 G), 35 G BROWN 6099, 20 G YELLOW 6002, 10 G RED 6014, 5 G GREEN 6086 (OR USE YOUR COLOR CHOICE OF LEFTOVER YARNS FOR THE CONTRAST COLORS)

NEEDLES: SET OF 4 OR 5 DPN U.S. SIZE 2.5 / 3 MM OR SIZE NEEDED TO OBTAIN GAUGE

GAUGE: 24 STS = 4 IN / 10 CM

STITCH COUNT: 44 STS AROUND HAND X APPROX 42 ROWS FOR LENGTH OF HAND

NOTE: To avoid long floats on the WS between color changes, twist the strand you are knitting with around the unused strand whenever there are more than 4 sts between color changes. Be careful not to pull the strand that floats.

RIGHT HAND MITTEN

With brown, CO 40 sts; divide onto dpn and join, being careful not to twist cast-on row. Work in k2, p2 ribbing for about 1½ in / 4 cm. Before beginning charted pattern for hand, knit 1 rnd with brown, and, at the same time, increase 4 sts evenly spaced around to 44 sts.

Now begin working charted pattern for right hand mitten. On the rnd above the black line on the chart, place the 7 sts underlined with black onto a holder for thumb and then CO 7 new sts over the gap following the pattern on the chart (CO with backward loop method) = 44 sts around.

Continue in charted pattern to top of mitten. Try on mitten to make sure it will be long enough – it should reach the top of the little finger. If necessary work a few more rounds before shaping. Always work decreases with brown. Decrease on each side of the single stitch at the sides of mitten. Work dec at right side (just after dividing line at side) of front (back) with ssk or sl 1-k1-psso; on the left side (before dividing line), k2tog. When 4 sts remain, cut yarn and pull tail through rem sts.

THUMB

Place the 7 sts from holder onto ndl and knit them with brown; next, pick up and knit 9 sts into CO row at top of thumbhole (use a crochet hook to pick up sts if necessary): 7 + 9 = 16 sts for thumb. Knit around in stockinette. Try on mitten to make sure thumb is long enough – it should reach to middle of thumbnail. If necessary, work a few more rounds before shaping top. Shape top of thumb as for top of mitten, decreasing at each side. When 2-4 sts remain, cut yarn and pull tail through rem sts.

LEFT HAND MITTEN

Work as for right hand making sure that you follow the chart for Left Hand.

FINISHING

Weave in all tails neatly on WS. See page 25 for information on garment care.

Squirrel and Hare

SIZE: ADULT
YARN: ASK HIFA 2 (SPORT, 100% WOOL, 344 YDS / 315 M, 100 G), 50 G BROWN 6099, 25 G YELLOW 6094, 10 G RED 6071, 10 G GREEN 6023
NEEDLES: SET OF 4 OR 5 DPN U.S. SIZE 2.5 / 3 MM OR SIZE NEEDED TO OBTAIN GAUGE
GAUGE: 24 STS = 4 IN / 10 CM
STITCH COUNT: 55 STS AROUND HAND X APPROX 60 ROWS FOR LENGTH OF HAND

NOTE: To avoid long floats on the WS between color changes, twist the strand you are knitting with around the unused strand whenever there are more than 4 sts between color changes. Be careful not to pull the strand that floats.

RIGHT HAND MITTEN

With brown, CO 44 sts; divide onto dpn and join, being careful not to twist cast-on row. Work in k2, p2 ribbing for about 2½-2¾ in / 6-7 cm. Before beginning charted pattern for hand, knit 1 rnd with brown, and, at the same time, increase 1 st to 45 sts.

Now begin working charted pattern for right hand mitten. On rnd 5 of hand, begin thumb gusset: K1, pm, M1, pm. Use M1 to increase for the extra sts for the thumb gusset, knitting into the inc on the following rnd. Increase on rnds as indicated on chart until there are 13 sts for thumb gusset.

Annemor V527

On the rnd above the red line on the chart, remove markers, place the 13 sts underlined with red onto a holder for thumb and then CO 11 new sts following the pattern on the chart (CO with backward loop method) = 55 sts around.

Continue in charted pattern to top of mitten. Try on mitten to make sure it will be long enough – it should reach the top of the little finger. If necessary work a few more rounds before shaping. Always work decreases with brown. Decrease on each side of the single stitch up each side of mitten. Work dec at right side (just after dividing line at side) of front (back) with ssk or sl 1-k1-psso; on the left side (before dividing line), k2tog. When 4 sts remain, cut yarn and pull tail through rem sts.

THUMB
Place the 13 sts from holder onto ndl and knit them with brown; next, pick up and knit 15 sts into CO row at top of thumbhole (use a crochet hook to pick up sts if necessary): 13 + 15 = 28 sts for thumb. On the next rnd, dec 1 st at each side to avoid holes and for correct stitch count: 13 + 13 = 26 sts. Knit around in stockinette. Try on mitten to make sure thumb is long enough – it should reach to middle of thumbnail. If necessary, work a few more rounds before shaping top. Shape top of thumb as for top of mitten, decreasing at each side. When 2-4 sts remain, cut yarn and pull tail through rem sts.

LEFT HAND MITTEN
Work as for right hand making sure that you follow the chart for Left Hand.

FINISHING
Weave in all tails neatly on WS. See page 25 for information on garment care.

SQUIRRELS FOR CHILD SIZE

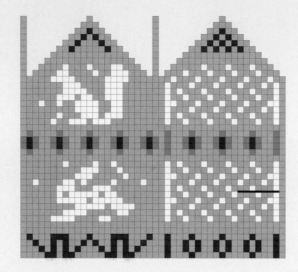

RIGHT HAND

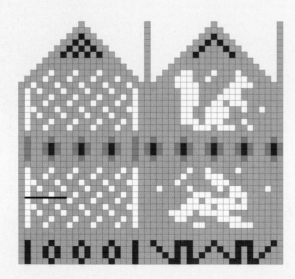

LEFT HAND

SQUIRRELS FOR ADULT SIZE

RIGHT HAND

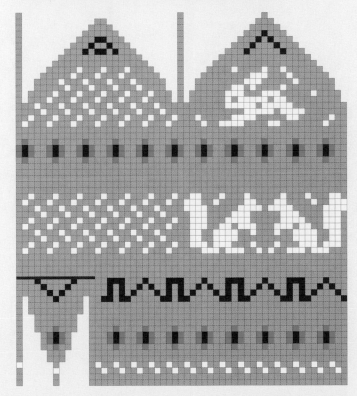

LEFT HAND

The Lord's Supper

The little border around the wrist is called a rose garland or rosary. Even after Lutheran education was instituted, people still prayed the rosary to the saints. That had to be done secretly because it was forbidden. In the Christian belief Jesus is often symbolized by a rose. The rose at the center of this glove (formed as on typical Norwegian waffles) is a variation of the communion wafer that reminds us of the bread Jesus shared at the Last Supper. It has also been said that the bottom part of the heart stands for the Greek letter alpha and the top for omega – the beginning and the end. The anchor shape in the middle stands for hope. The cross at the center is faith and the circle around it is eternity. The three-petal lily is the Holy Trinity. This grouping of symbols represents Jesus' departing words to his disciples as written in an old Bible translation.

SIZE: MAN'S
YARN: ASK HIFA 2 (SPORT, 100% WOOL, 344 YDS / 315 M, 100 G), 70 G WHITE 6057, 50 G BLACK 6053
NEEDLES: SET OR 4 OR 5 DPN U.S. SIZE 1.5 / 2.5 MM OR SIZE NEEDED TO OBTAIN GAUGE. IF DESIRED DPN ONE SIZE SMALL FOR KNITTING FINGERS
GAUGE: 28 STS = 4 IN / 10 CM
STITCH COUNT: 72 STS AROUND HAND

NOTE: To avoid long floats on the WS between color changes, twist the strand you are knitting with around the unused strand whenever there are more than 4 sts between color changes. Be careful not to pull the strand that floats.

RIGHT HAND GLOVE
With white, CO 60 sts; divide onto dpn and join,
being careful not to twist cast-on row. Work 3 rnds of k1, p1 ribbing and then knit 1 rnd with white. Next, attach black and work the charted cuff pattern. Finish cuff by knitting 1 rnd with white, increasing 2 sts evenly spaced around to 62 sts. Knit 1 more round with white.

Now begin working charted pattern for right hand glove. Use M1 to increase for the extra sts for the thumb gusset, knitting into the inc on the following rnd. On rnd 2, begin thumb gusset: k6 pm, M1, k1, M1, pm. On the next rnd, knit the new sts in pattern. Increase on rnds as indicated on chart until there are 15 sts for thumb gusset.

On the rnd above the red line on the chart, remove markers, place the 15 sts underlined with red onto a holder for thumb and then CO 15 new sts follow-

Annemor V899

ing the pattern on the chart (CO with backward loop method) = 72 sts around.

Continue in charted pattern to the base of the fingers. Place hand sts on a holder while you knit the thumb. Use a needle 1 U.S. size / 0.5 mm smaller than for hand.

THUMB
Place the 15 sts from holder onto ndl and then, in pattern, pick up and knit 17 sts into CO row at top of thumbhole (use a crochet hook to pick up sts if necessary): 15 + 17 = 32 sts for thumb. Knit the thumb following charted pattern to thumb shaping. Try on the glove to make sure the thumb is long enough (it should reach middle of thumbnail); work more rounds as needed for desired thumb length. Shape top of thumb as follows: decrease at right side of front (back) with ssk or sl 1-k1-psso; on the left side, k2tog. When 8 sts rem, cut yarn and pull tail through rem sts.

INDEX FINGER
Place 10 sts from the back of the hand + 3 side sts + 8 sts from palm onto ndls and CO 4 sts with

backwards loop method at base of middle finger = 25 sts total. Knit following chart for index finger until finger is desired length and then shape top as for thumb.

MIDDLE FINGER
Place 7 sts from the back of the hand onto dpn, pick up and knit 4 sts from cast-on at base of index finger, place 9 sts from palm onto ndl, and CO 5 sts with backwards loop method at base of ring finger = 25 sts total. Knit following chart for middle finger until finger is desired length and then shape top as for thumb.

RING FINGER
Place 7 sts from the back of the hand onto dpn, pick up and knit 5 sts from cast-on at base of middle finger, place 9 sts from palm onto ndl, and CO 4 sts with backwards loop method at base of little finger = 25 sts total. Knit following chart for ring finger until finger is desired length and then shape top as for thumb.

LITTLE FINGER
Place rem sts = 7 from back of hand + 3 side sts + 9 sts from palm and then pick up and knit 5 sts along cast-on at base of ring finger = total of 24 sts. Knit following chart for little finger until finger is desired length and the shape top as for thumb.

LEFT HAND GLOVE
Work as for right hand making sure that you follow the chart for Left Hand and place thumb and fingers correctly.

FINISHING
Weave in all tails neatly on WS. See page 25 for information on garment care.

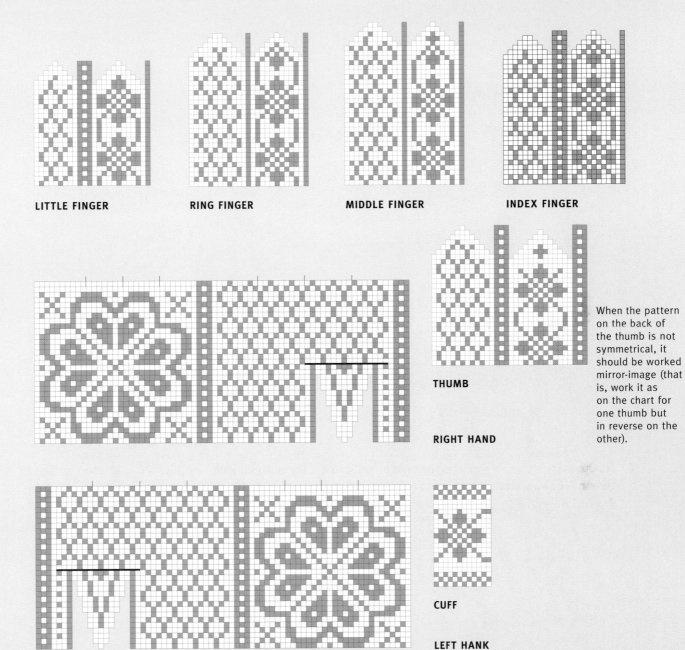

LITTLE FINGER

RING FINGER

MIDDLE FINGER

INDEX FINGER

THUMB

RIGHT HAND

When the pattern on the back of the thumb is not symmetrical, it should be worked mirror-image (that is, work it as on the chart for one thumb but in reverse on the other).

CUFF

LEFT HANK

Moose at Sundown

Evergreens represent eternal life because they are always green and the sun is eternal, life-giving energy. This glove is the "Moose at Sundown" motif artfully translated to knitting. The glove follows the Selbu tradition with its construction, motifs, and color choice. It is totally up to you to follow the traditional color choice or to experiment with your own selection of colors.

SIZE: MAN'S
YARN: ASK HIFA 2 (SPORT, 100% WOOL, 344 YDS / 315 M, 100 G), 70 G WHITE 6057, 50 G BLACK 6053
NEEDLES: SET OR 4 OR 5 DPN U.S. SIZE 1.5 / 2.5 MM OR SIZE NEEDED TO OBTAIN GAUGE
GAUGE: 28 STS = 4 IN / 10 CM
STITCH COUNT: 79 STS AROUND HAND

NOTE: To avoid long floats on the WS between color changes, twist the strand you are knitting with around the unused strand whenever there are more than 4 sts between color changes. Be careful not to pull the strand that floats.

RIGHT HAND GLOVE
With white, CO 60 sts; divide onto dpn and join, being careful not to twist cast-on row. Work 3 rnds of k1, p1 ribbing and then knit 1 rnd with white. Next, attach black and work the charted cuff pattern. Finish cuff by knitting 1 rnd with white, increasing 9 sts evenly spaced around to 69 sts. Knit 1 more round with white.

Now begin working charted pattern for right hand glove. Use M1 to increase for the extra sts for the thumb gusset, knitting into the inc on the following rnd. On rnd 4, begin thumb gusset: k4, pm, M1, k1, M1, pm. On the next rnd, knit the new sts in pattern. Increase on rnds as indicated on chart until there are 15 sts for thumb gusset.
On the rnd above the red line on the chart, remove markers, place the 15 sts underlined with red onto a holder for thumb and then CO 13 new sts following the pattern on the chart (CO with backward loop method) = 72 sts around.

Continue in charted pattern to the base of the fingers. Place hand sts on a holder while you knit the thumb.

THUMB

Place the 15 sts from holder onto ndl and then, in pattern, pick up and knit 15 sts into CO row at top of thumbhole (use a crochet hook to pick up sts if necessary): 15 + 15 = 30 sts for thumb. Knit the thumb following charted pattern and, on the first rnd, k2tog at each side to avoid holes and for correct stitch count: 15 + 13 = 28 sts. Work following chart to thumb shaping. Try on the glove to make sure the thumb is long enough (it should reach middle of thumbnail); work more rounds as needed for desired thumb length. Shape top of thumb as follows: decrease at right side of front (back) with ssk or sl 1-k1-psso; on the left side, k2tog. When 4 sts rem, cut yarn and pull tail through rem sts.

INDEX FINGER

Place 11 sts from the back of the hand + 1 side st + 10 sts from palm onto ndls and CO 2 sts with backwards loop method at base of middle finger = 24 sts total. Knit following chart for index finger until finger is desired length and then shape top as for thumb.

MIDDLE FINGER

Place 9 sts from the back of the hand onto dpn, pick up and knit 3 sts from cast-on at base of index finger, place 9 sts from palm onto ndl, and CO 3 sts with backwards loop method at base of ring finger = 24 sts total. Knit following chart for middle finger until finger is desired length and then shape top as for thumb.

RING FINGER

Place 9 sts from the back of the hand onto dpn, pick up and knit 3 sts from cast-on at base of

Annemor V711.8

middle finger, place 9 sts from palm onto ndl, and CO 3 sts with backwards loop method at base of little finger = 24 sts total. Knit following chart for ring finger until finger is desired length and then shape top as for thumb.

LITTLE FINGER

Place rem sts = 9 from back of hand + 1 side st + 11 sts from palm and then pick up and knit 3 sts along cast-on at base of ring finger = total of 24 sts. Knit following chart for little finger until finger is desired length and the shape top as for thumb.

LEFT HAND GLOVE

Work as for right hand making sure that you follow the chart for Left Hand and place thumb and fingers correctly.

FINISHING

Weave in all tails neatly on WS. See page 25 for information on garment care.

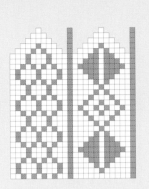  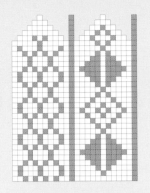

LITTLE FINGER **MIDDLE FINGER** **RING AND INDEX FINGERS**

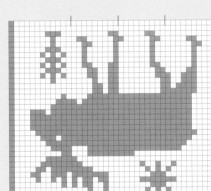 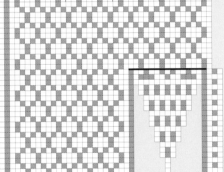 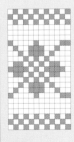

THUMB

RIGHT HAND GLOVE

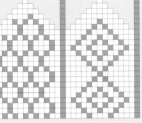

When the pattern on the back of the thumb is not symmetrical, it should be worked mirror-image (that is, work it as on the chart for one thumb but in re-verse on the other).

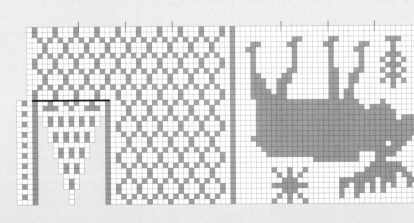

CUFF

LEFT HAND GLOVE

Dancing Grannies Mittens

These "Dancing Grannies Mittens" are my own design. They represent women's power with memories of the fight for women's rights, the hippie days, the goddesses of destiny, enticing lady dancers, troll women, and rock 'n' roll. I don't have any old mittens with this motif but I wanted to honor Annichen Sibbern for including the women dancers in the book *Norwegian Sweater Designs* that she published in 1929. In a later edition she wrote that the previous edition had sold out: "I hope and believe that these patterns – despite all the fashion trends – will always be used and preserved because they are good Norwegian art."

SIZE: WOMAN'S
YARN: ASK HIFA 2 (SPORT, 100% WOOL, 344 YDS / 315 M, 100 G), 75 G LIGHT (MC), 25 G DARK (CC) (USE YOUR CHOICE OF CHEERFUL COLORS FOR YOUR DANCING GRANNIES)
NEEDLES: SET OR 4 OR 5 DPN U.S. SIZE 1.5 / 2.5 MM OR SIZE NEEDED TO OBTAIN GAUGE
GAUGE: 28 STS = 4 IN / 10 CM
STITCH COUNT: 64 STS AROUND HAND X APPROX 62 ROWS FOR LENGTH OF HAND

NOTE: To avoid long floats on the WS between color changes, twist the strand you are knitting with around the unused strand whenever there are more than 4 sts between color changes. Be careful not to pull the strand that floats.

RIGHT HAND MITTEN

With CC, CO 56 sts. Divide sts onto dpn and join, being careful not to twist cast-on row. Work 1 rnd in k2, p2 ribbing and then cut CC and add MC; continue in k2, p2 ribbing for approx 2½-2¾ in / 6-7 cm. Next, knit 1 rnd with MC, increasing 2 sts evenly spaced around to 58 sts. Knit 1 more round and then add CC.

Now begin working charted patterns for right hand mitten – work the border pattern (with a round of MC before and after the two charted rows) and then work the charted hand pattern. Use M1 to increase for the extra sts for the thumb gusset, knitting into the inc on the following rnd. On rnd 4, begin thumb gusset: k6, pm, M1, k3, M1, pm. On

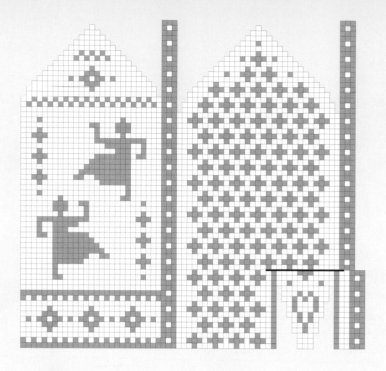

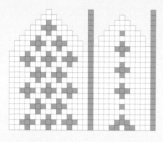

THUMB

RIGHT HAND

▨▨▨▨

BORDER ABOVE CUFF

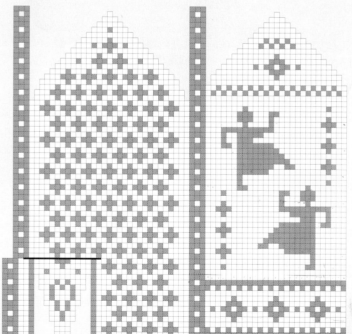

LEFT HAND

the next rnd, knit the new sts in pattern. Increase on rnds as indicated on chart until there are 15 sts for thumb gusset.

On the rnd above the red line on the chart, remove markers, place the 15 sts underlined with red onto a holder for thumb and then CO 15 new sts following the pattern on the chart (CO with backward loop method) = 64 sts around.

Continue in charted pattern to top of mitten. Have the person who will wear the mitten try it on to make sure it fits. Always work decreases with MC. Decrease on each side of the contrast color columns up the sides of mitten. Work dec at right side of front (back) with ssk or sl 1-k1-psso; on the left side, k2tog. When 8 sts remain, cut yarn and pull tail through rem sts.

THUMB
Place the 15 sts from holder onto ndl and then, in pattern, pick up and knit 15 sts into CO row at top of thumbhole (use a crochet hook to pick up sts if necessary): 15 + 15 = 30 sts for thumb. Work following charted pattern for thumb, and, on the first rnd, k2tog at each side to avoid holes and for correct stitch count: 15 + 13 = 28 sts. Work until thumb is desired length; if necessary, work a few more rounds before shaping. Shape top of thumb as for top of mitten.

LEFT HAND MITTEN
Work as for right hand making sure that you follow the chart for Left Hand.

FINISHING
Weave in all tails neatly on WS. See page 25 for information on garment care.

One Mitten is a Pattern Treasure Trove

This section of the book is for anyone who wants to follow their own imagination and creativity. You can choose to follow the charts and instructions that I constructed for the hand knit garments from my rag pile or you can take inspiration from them to make your own variations. Whether you want to knit a mitten or another garment, the patterns in this book come from our Norwegian traditional heritage and belong to a universal language of symbols.

MAKING A PATTERN REPEAT

When you are in the process of designing a pattern, you can isolate one part of a motif from a mitten or glove. Because this motif can be repeated, the pattern sequence is called a "repeat."

If you count out the repeat on graph paper, you can see how many stitches are needed for the width and height.

The next step is to find out how many stitches you need for your garment in your size. If you want to knit a headband, for example, you have to calculate how many stitches you need around your head. You can figure this out by measuring the number of inches/centimeters around your head. When you choose the yarn, the ball band usually recommends a needle size for that yarn and how many stitches and rows are in a 4 x 4 in / 10 x 10 cm square. If you use stash or leftover yarns, you should knit a gauge swatch to check the number of stitches and rows per inch/centimeter for your garment.

When you know how many stitches are needed for the total, you can then apportion the total into the repeats.

A pattern from a mitten can be repeated and the border can be added. The result can be used for a headband, sock legs, etc.

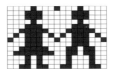 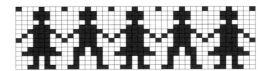

*With different color combinations and background these border panels
can be knit in any number of variations for a pillow top.*

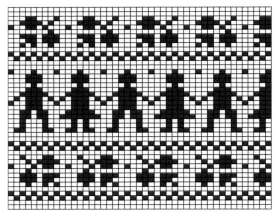

What if the numbers don't "add up," and you end up with a total that has too few or too many stitches in relation to the stitch count you need? If it is only a few stitches, it doesn't matter much. If it is a number of stitches, which would make the headband too big or too small, you have several options. The easiest can be to work the pattern all around the headband, or to add a little star or another motif as a finishing at the back where the extra stitches are. You can also add or subtract space between elements in the pattern repeat.

After you've had some practice, you'll be able to combine patterns and create new pattern repeats. You can repeat the same pattern or you could mirror image it to get the stitch count to match the total number you need for your garment. You'll soon be able to choose some motifs and make your own arrangements from the pattern treasure chest in this book.

BORDERS AND SMALL MOTIFS

If you find a mitten with a motif you like, you can use it to decorate both gloves and wrist warmers. You can choose how much patterning you want on the fingers but be sure and select only small designs. For wrist warmers, the possibilities are greater – you can choose freely among borders, animal figures or overall patterns from traditional pattern sources.

MITTEN FORMS FOR HATS AND SOCKS

The shape of a mitten can also be used when you want to knit hats and socks. Select a basic pattern and adjust the pattern repeat to fit the total stitch count. You can repeat the same pattern, mirror-image it, or use different colors to create a variation. The possibilities are endless, and the treasure chest of traditional motifs is common property. The power of creation is in your hands!

Hat: **Dancing Hat**

Here's a suggestion for how a mitten shape can be used for a hat.

The pattern shown here is large enough for half a hat.
Measure the size of the hat you want to knit and make sure the stitch count is appropriate for the yarn, needles, and pattern repeats.

Use the mitten form x 6 repeats (the picture shows 3 repeats) and adjust the pattern if necessary.
The hat can be worked with a folded up brim. You can begin with a short ribbed border but remember that the panel of dancers must be knitted from the top down in that case (begin reading chart at top left corner of panel). After all the charted rows have been knit, purl one round for the foldline. Now work with a single color a little past the foldline. Decide how long you want it. Now turn the hat inside out so the side facing you reverses from stockinette to reverse stockinette. Work the charted panel for the crown and then shape the top as for a mitten.

If you don't want a doubled brim, you can make a little ribbed border and then begin knitting from the bottom right hand corner of the chart. Continue onto the chart for the crown and shape the top as for a mitten. You can use a single ply of the knitting yarn to sew any little holes when finishing.

You can experiment by adding other borders or varying the colors.

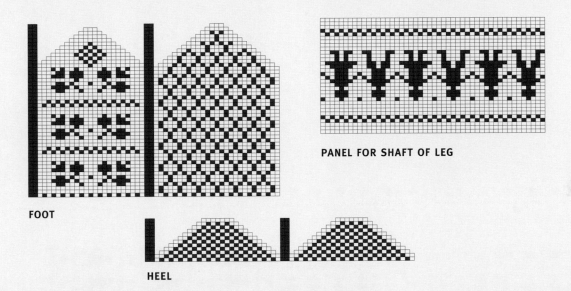

FOOT

PANEL FOR SHAFT OF LEG

HEEL

Border panels can be knitted on a doubled cuff for a sock leg. You can begin with a short ribbed border. The panel for the cuff must be knitted from the top down (begin reading chart at top left corner of panel). After all the charted rows have been knit, purl one round for the foldline. Now work with a single color until just below the panel and border. Decide on how long you want it. Now turn the piece inside out so that the side facing you reverses from stockinette to reverse stockinette (the purl side).

If you don't want a doubled cuff, you can work a short ribbed edge and then begin knitting from the bottom right hand corner of the chart as for the cuff of a mitten. You can decide on the length of this section between the cuff and the foot.

The foot should be knitted as for the hand of a mitten. In the same way as you set off stitches for a thumb, you set aside stitches for a heel. Knit in a waste yarn where the black line is between the side stitches on the underside of the foot. This is called a "provisional heel". When the foot is finished you remove the waste yarn and place the stitches onto the knitting needles. Divide the stitches onto 4 or 5 dpn and knit the heel around and then shape as shown on the chart. Join the last row of stitches with Kitchener stitch.

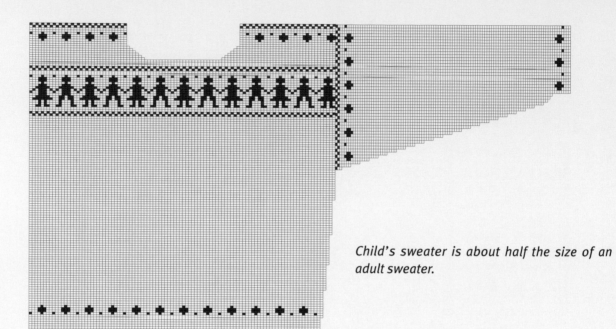

Child's sweater is about half the size of an adult sweater.

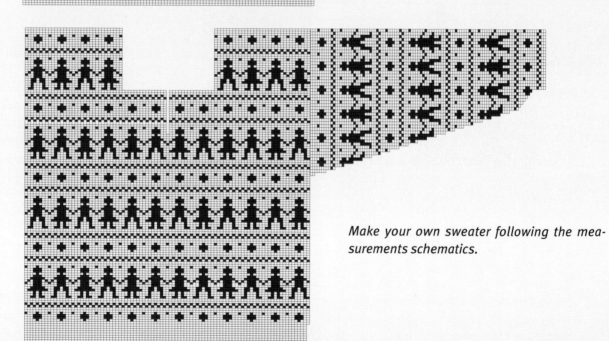

Make your own sweater following the measurements schematics.

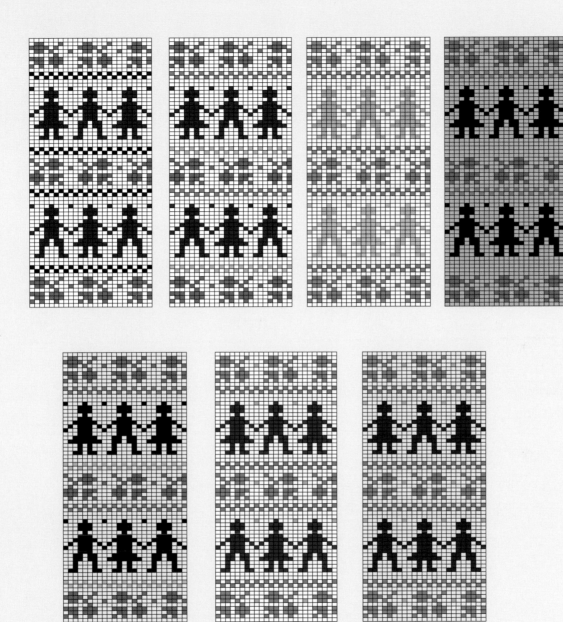

Colors and panels can be varied as much as you like.

MEASUREMENT SCHEMATICS FOR SWEATERS
WITH STANDARD SIZES AND A SCHEMATIC FOR YOUR OWN MEASUREMENTS AND STITCH COUNT.

MEASUREMENTS APPROX	SMALL	MEDIUM	LARGE	X LARGE	XX LARGE
Length shoulder to hip	60 cm	65 cm	70 cm	75 cm	80 cm
	23 ¾ in	25 ½ in	27 ½ in	29 ½ in	31 ½ in
Length shoulder to waist	40 cm	45 cm	50 cm	55 cm	60 cm
	15 ¾ in	17 ¾ in	19 ¾ in	21 ¾ in	23 ¾ in
Circumference chest	110 CM	120 CM	130 CM	10 CM	150 CM
	43 ½ in	47 ¼ in	51 ¼ in	55 ¼ in	59 in
Front + back	55 + 55 cm	60 x 60 cm	65 + 65 cm	70 + 70 cm	75 + 75 cm
	21¾ + 21¾ in	23¾ + 23¾ in	25½ + 25½ in	27½ + 27½ in	29½ + 29½ in
Sleeve length excluding cuff	45 cm	45 cm	50 cm	50 cm	55 cm
	17¾ in	17¾ in	19¾ in	19¾ in	21¾ in
Cuff length	5 cm	5 cm	5 cm	5 cm	5 cm
	2 in	2 in	2 in	2 in	2 in
Width of lower sleeve	20 cm	25 cm	30 cm	35 cm	35 cm
	8 in	9 ¾ in	11 ¾ in	13 ¾ in	13 ¾ in
Width of upper sleeve	50 cm	55 cm	60 cm	65 cm	70 cm
	19 ¾ in	21 ¾ in	23 ¾ in	25 ½ in	27 ½ in

MEASUREMENTS APPROX	1 YEAR	3 YEARS	6 YEARS	9 YEARS	12 YEARS
Length shoulder to hip	30 cm	35 cm	40 cm	45 cm	50 cm
	11 ¾ in	13 ¾ in	15 ¾ in	17 ¾ in	19 ¾ in
Length shoulder to waist	20 cm	25 cm	30 cm	32 cm	35 cm
	8 in	9 ¾ in	11 ¾ in	12 ¾ in	13 ¾ in
Circumference chest	60 cm	70 cm	80 cm	90 cm	100 cm
	23 ¾ in	27 ½ in	31 ½ in	35 ½ in	39 ½ in
Front + back	30 + 30 cm	35 + 35 cm	40 + 40 cm	45 + 45 cm	50 + 50 cm
	11¾+ 11¾ in	13¾ + 13¾ in	15¾ + 15¾ in	17¾ + 17¾ in	19¾ + 19¾ in
Cuff length	2 cm	3 cm	3 cm	4 cm	5 cm
	¾ in	1¼ in	1¼ in	1½ in	2 in
Sleeve length excluding cuff	20 cm	25 cm	30 cm	35 cm	40 cm
	8 in	9¾ in	11¾ in	13¾ in	15¾ in
Width of lower Sleeve	15 cm	20 cm	20 cm	22 cm	22 cm
	6 in	8 in	8 in	8¾ in	8¾ in
Width of upper Sleeve	25 cm	30 cm	35 cm	40 cm	45 cm
	9¾ in	11¾ in	13¾ in	15¾ in	17¾ in

INDIVIDUAL	MEASUREMENTS APPROX	YOUR MEASUREMENTS		YOUR STITCH COUNT
Length shoulder to hip	in/cm	x rows per in/cm	=	rows
Length shoulder to waist	in/cm	x rows per in/cm	=	rows
Chest circumference	in/cm	x stitches per in/cm	=	stitches
Sleeve length excluding cuff	in/cm	x stitches per in/cm	=	stitches
Cuff length	in/cm	x rows per in/cm	=	rows
Width of lower sleeve	in/cm	x rows per in/cm	=	rows
Width of upper sleeve	in/cm	x stitches per in/cm	=	stitches
Width of upper sleeve	in/cm	x stitches per in/cm	=	stitches
Bottom edge of body, length	in/cm	x rows per in/cm	=	rows

STANDARD MEASUREMENTS FOR MITTEN AND GLOVE CONSTRUCTION

MITTENS APPROX IN/CM	LENGTH RIBBED CUFF	CUFF TO THUMBHOLE	THUMBHOLE TO MITTEN TIP	THUMBHOLE TO THUMB TIP	HAND WIDTH	THUMB WIDTH
MAN'S MITTEN	8 CM 10 CM	6 CM	15 CM	7.5 CM	10.5 CM	4 CM
	3 ¼ IN 4 IN	2 ½ IN	6 IN	3 IN	4 IN	1 ½ IN
WOMAN'S	8 CM 10 CM	5 CM	14 CM	7 CM	9 CM	3.5 CM
	3 ¼ IN 4 IN	2 IN	5 ½ IN	2 ¾ IN	3 ½ IN	1 ¼ IN
BOY/GIRL'S MITTEN	6 CM 7 CM	4 CM	13 CM	6.5 CM	9 CM	3.5 CM
	2 ½ IN 4 IN	1 ¾ IN	5 ¼ IN	2 ½ IN	3 ½ IN	1 ¼ IN
SMALL CHILD'S MITTEN	4 CM 5 CM	3 CM	9 CM	5 CM	7-8 CM	3 CM
	1 ¾ IN 2 IN	1 ¼ IN	3 ½ IN	2 IN	2 ¾-3 ¼ IN	1 ¼ IN

GLOVES APPROX IN/CM			THUMBHOLE TO FINGERS LENGTH/WIDTH				INDEX FINGER LENGTH/WIDTH	MIDDLE FINGER LENGTH/WIDTH	RING FINGER LENGTH/WIDTH	LITTLE FINGER LENGTH/WIDTH
MAN'S	8-10	6 CM	7 CM	7-8 CM	10,5 CM	4 CM 3,5 CM	8 CM 3,5 CM	9,5 CM 3,5 CM	9 CM 3 CM	6,5 CM
	3 ¼-4 IN	2 ½ IN	2 ¾ IN	2 ¾-3 ¼ IN	4 IN	1 ¾ IN	3 ¼/1 ¼ IN	3 ¾/1 ¼ IN	3 ½/1 ¼ IN	2 ½/1 ¼ IN
WOMAN'S	8-10	5 CM	6 CM	7 CM	9 CM	3,5 CM 3 CM	7 CM 3,5 CM	8,5 CM 3 CM	7,5 CM 2,5 CM	6 CM
	3 ¼-4 IN	2 IN	2 ½ IN	2 ¾ IN	3 ½ IN	1 ¼ IN	2 ¾/1 ¼ IN	3 ¼/1 ¼ IN	3/1 ¼ IN	2 ½/1 IN

IF THERE IS A RIBBED CUFF, IT IS OFTEN A LITTLE LONGER THAN A PATTERNED CUFF.

STANDARD GLOVE LENGTHS:

MAN'S APPROX 8 ¼ IN / 21 CM   WOMAN'S APPROX 7 ½ IN / 19 CM   BOY/GIRL'S 6 ¾ IN / 17 CM   SMALL CHILD'S 5 ½ IN / 14 CM

Resources

LEXICONS AND SYMBOL DICTIONARIES

Binder, Pearl. *Magic Symbols of the World*. Hamlyn, 1972.

Ferguson, George. *Sign and Symbols in Christian Art*. Oxford University Press, 1981.

BOOKS AND MAGAZINES

Bennet, Helen M. *The Shetland Hand Knitting Industry. I: Scottish Textile History*. Aberdeen, 1987.

Don, Sarah. *Fair Isle Knitting*. Dover, 2007.

Fossnes, Heidi. *Håndplagg, votter till bunader og folkedrakter [Handcoverings for National and Folk Costumes]*. Damm, 2003 (available from nordicfiberarts.com).

Gravjord, Ingebjørg. *Votten in norsk tradisjon [Traditional Norwegian Mittens]*. Landbruksforlaget, 1986 (available from www.saterglantan.se)

Shea, Terri. *Selbuvotter: Biography of a Knitting Tradition*. Spinningwheel, 2007 (www.selbuvotter.com).

Sibbern, Annichen. *Norwegian Knitting Designs: Charts and Patterns for Traditional Designs*. Seattle WI: Spinningwheel, 2011.

Thomas, Mary. *Mary Thomas' Knitting Book*, Dover, 1972.

Nordic Fiber Arts
4 Cutts Road
Durham, NH 03824
603-868-1196
info@nordicfiberarts.com
www.nordicfoberarts.com

Hifa **Hillesvåg Ullvarefabrikk**

Ask Hifa 2 – 100% pure new wool

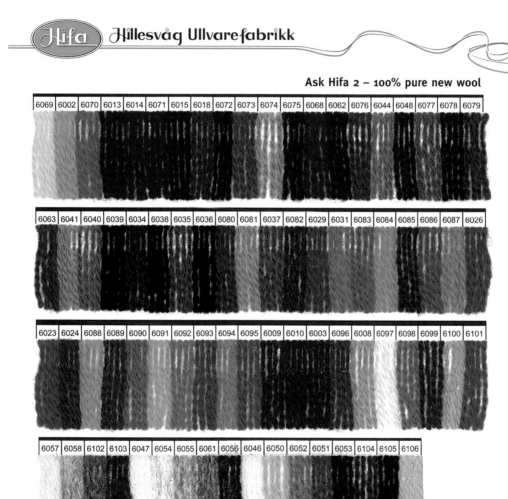

6069	6002	6070	6013	6014	6071	6015	6018	6072	6073	6074	6075	6068	6062	6076	6044	6048	6077	6078	6079

6063	6041	6040	6039	6034	6038	6035	6036	6080	6081	6037	6082	6029	6031	6083	6084	6085	6086	6087	6026

6023	6024	6088	6089	6090	6091	6092	6093	6094	6095	6009	6010	6003	6096	6008	6097	6098	6099	6100	6101

6057	6058	6102	6103	6047	6054	6055	6061	6056	6046	6050	6052	6051	6053	6104	6105	6106